Higher Education, Leadership and Women
Vice Chancellors

Palgrave Studies in Gender and Education

Series Editor:

Yvette Taylor, London South Bank University, UK

This series aims to provide a comprehensive space for an increasingly diverse and complex area of interdisciplinary social science research: Gender and Education. As the field of women and gender studies is rapidly developing and becoming 'internationalised' – as with traditional social science disciplines of sociology, educational studies, social geography etc. – there is greater need for a dynamic, global series that plots emerging definitions and debates, and monitors critical complexities of gender and education. This series will have an explicitly feminist approach and orientation, attending to key theoretical and methodological debates, and ensuring a continued conversation and relevance within the interdisciplinary and long-standing 'Gender and Education' field.

The series will be better able to combine renewed and revitalised feminist research methods and theories with emergent and salient public and policy issues. These include pre-compulsory and post-compulsory education, 'early years' and 'life long' education; educational (dis)engagements of pupils, students and staff; trajectories and intersectional inequalities including race, class, sexuality, age, disability; policy and practice across educational landscapes; diversity and difference, including institutional (schools, colleges, universities), locational and embodied (in 'teacher'-'learner' positions); varied global activism in and beyond the classroom and the 'public university'; educational technologies and transitions and the (ir)relevance of (in)formal educational settings; emergent educational mainstreams and margins. In operating a critical approach to 'gender and education', the series recognises the importance of probing beyond the boundaries of specific territorial-legislative domains in order to develop a more international, intersectional focus. In addressing varied conceptual and methodological questions, the series combines an intersectional focus on competing – and sometimes colliding – strands of educational provisioning, equality and 'diversity', as well as providing insightful reflections of the continuing critical shift of gender and feminism within (and beyond) the academy.

Titles include:

Anne Harris and Emily Gray
QUEER TEACHERS, IDENTITY AND PERFORMATIVITY

Emily F. Henderson
GENDER PEDAGOGY

Paula Burkinshaw
HIGHER EDUCATION, LEADERSHIP AND WOMEN VICE CHANCELLORS
Fitting into Communities of Practice of Masculinities

Palgrave Studies in Gender and Education
Series Standing Order ISBN 978–1–137–45634–2 Hardback
978–1–137–45635–9 Paperback
(*outside North America only*)

You can receive future titles in this series as they are published by placing a standing order. Please contact your bookseller or, in case of difficulty, write to us at the address below with your name and address, the title of the series and the ISBN quoted above.

Customer Services Department, Macmillan Distribution Ltd, Houndmills, Basingstoke, Hampshire RG21 6XS, England

---

Higher Education, Leadership and Women Vice Chancellors

Fitting into Communities of Practice of Masculinities

Paula Burkinshaw

University of Leeds, UK

First published 2015 by
PALGRAVE MACMILLAN

Palgrave Macmillan in the UK is an imprint of Macmillan Publishers Limited, registered in England, company number 785998, of Houndmills, Basingstoke, Hampshire RG21 6XS.

Palgrave Macmillan in the US is a division of St Martin's Press LLC, 175 Fifth Avenue, New York, NY 10010.

Palgrave Macmillan is the global academic imprint of the above companies and has companies and representatives throughout the world.

Palgrave® and Macmillan® are registered trademarks in the United States, the United Kingdom, Europe and other countries.

ISBN 978–1–137–44403–5

This book is printed on paper suitable for recycling and made from fully managed and sustained forest sources. Logging, pulping and manufacturing processes are expected to conform to the environmental regulations of the country of origin.

A catalogue record for this book is available from the British Library.

Library of Congress Cataloging-in-Publication Data
Burkinshaw, Paula.
  Higher education, leadership and women vice chancellors : fitting in to communities of practice of masculinities / Paula Burkinshaw.
    pages   cm
  Summary: "Why are there so few women vice chancellors in UK higher education? In this book, Paula Burkinshaw explores the contemporary conversation around the 'missing women at the top' across UK society through in-depth interviews with the (hitherto) silent voices of women vice chancellors. These women have successfully negotiated with and navigated the gendered leadership cultures of higher education throughout their careers and speak of the masculine communities of their workplaces. Advocating the need to achieve a critical mass of women at the top, this book suggests there is still much to be done in the higher education sphere" — Provided by publisher.
  ISBN 978–1–137–44403–5 (hardback)
  1. Education, Higher—Administration.   2. Educational leadership.
  3. Women college administrators.   4. Women in higher education.
  5. Sex discrimination in higher education.   6. Masculinity—
  Social aspects.   7. Organizational change.   I. Title.
  LB2341.B748 2015
  378.0082—dc23   2015002336

Contents

Preface

It's still seen as odd. Bit like that dancing cats. It's not how they do it; it's that they do it at all. (16)[1]

This book represents a milestone along the way of a research journey during which I have been exploring the underrepresentation of women at vice chancellor level in UK higher education through the lens of gendered leadership cultures. Whilst I was working as a leadership development professional in universities, for ten years prior to embarking upon my PhD, I became passionate about the underrepresentation of women in leadership generally, and began asking myself 'where are the women?' and 'why are there so few women vice chancellors?'

As higher education is not alone in suffering from a lack of diversity in leadership, I have set the context of my research within the growing conversation about 'the missing women at the top' across all sectors, within and beyond education.

My study has been underpinned by a theoretical framework around 'leadership communities of practice of masculinities', by my epistemological feminism and by my agenda for change. Consequently, my review of the literature has searched for previous published work around gendered leadership cultures, feminist methodology and the critical mass conversation, and critical reflexivity around this literature has fundamentally informed my work.

As a result of their underrepresentation at the top of higher education, the voices of women vice chancellors have invariably been silent and strange (unusual), so my study seeks *their* views about the 'missing women' in higher education leadership. This book provides an insight into my interviews with 18 women who lead higher education institutions and discusses this data in relation to the literature and theoretical framework.

Three common themes emerged during my research study, namely: the negotiation and navigation of gendered leadership cultures; higher

---

[1] Whenever I use a quotation from my interview data, I identify that interview by a number from 1 to 18 and I explain more about my decision to do this in Chapter 3.

education leadership communities of practice of masculinities; and achieving a critical mass of women at the top. Throughout the book, these themes provide cohesion, make sense of what I have been learning and clarify my contribution to knowledge about this important issue.

Acknowledgements

It has been a great privilege for me that my research exploring the missing women in higher education leadership has brought me into close contact with so many wonderful women, as both a researcher and a practitioner. The richness of this study is without doubt due to the generosity of these women, particularly the 18 women research participants who freely gave me their time and trusted me with their experiences. I am especially grateful to all the women involved in this study and really hope that I have done justice to their contributions.

I cannot thank my family enough for their overwhelming support and encouragement throughout the years that I was studying for my PhD. Tackling such a major research project at my time of life was particularly challenging and I would not have succeeded without the care and consideration of my very special family.

This book is dedicated to my parents who both died prematurely so they missed out not only on many years of pleasure from grandchildren they hardly knew but also on my emerging career. They would have been immensely proud of my achievements and it is with great sorrow that I now thank them both for their unconditional love and lifelong inspiration.

Abbreviations

BERA	British Educational Research Association
CEO	Chief Executive Officer
CIM	Chartered Institute of Management
CIPD	Chartered Institute of Personnel and Development
CUC	Committee of University Chairs
ECU	Equality Challenge Unit
EU	European Union
EHRC	Equality and Human Rights Commission
FTSE	Financial Times Stock Exchange
GDP	Gross Domestic Product
HE	Higher Education
HEFCE	Higher Education Funding Council
HESA	Higher Education Statistics Agency
HR	Human Resources
IMF	International Monetary Fund
LFHE	Leadership Foundation for Higher Education
MP	Member of Parliament
ONS	Office for National Statistics
PA	Professional Assistant
SRHE	Society for Research in Higher Education
STEMM	Science, Technology, Engineering, Mathematics and Medicine
THE	Times Higher Education
TUC	Trades Union Council
UCEA	University and College Employers Association
UCU	University and College Union
UK	United Kingdom
UUK	Universities UK

1
Introduction

1.1 Background to this research

Women are significantly underrepresented in senior public and private appointments across the UK such that, on average, women hold 26 per cent of top jobs in the public sector and 10 per cent of top jobs in business (Commission, 2011). According to the Equality and Human Rights Commission landmark Sex and Power report, there are 5,400 women missing from senior appointments in all sectors across the UK (Commission, 2011). Fundamentally, Britain is a country largely run by men (Coalition, 2013).

Women's representation in senior appointments is important (in higher education and beyond) for four fundamental reasons. First: social justice, which 'recognises that people are not treated equally and implies intervention to change institutions and society towards being more just' (Coleman and Glover, 2010) (p:7). Second: equity and parity, to tackle the gender pay and opportunity gap (UCU, 2013, Davidson and Burke, 2011, Prosser, 2006, Ford, 2011). Third: quality, to enhance the quality of higher education leadership it is crucial not to overlook any of the female academic population (Rice, 2014). And last: the economy and business, whereby nationally there is a growing urgency to the conversation about gender equality in leadership, such that the professions have become much more attuned to the business case for equality, diversity and inclusion (Desvaux et al., 2010, Walby, 2011, Phillips, 2012, CIPD, 2005, Deloitte, 2011, Foundation, 2006, Department for Business, 2013). Interestingly, recent research indicates that vice chancellors are most motivated by the social justice and quality rationale in their ambitions for gender equality in their institutions (Ross and Schneider, 2014). So far the corporate sector has avoided the imposition of quotas for the representation of women at board level by seeking to ensure that government targets are met (Davies, 2014). This target is now being reinforced by an inquiry into board appointments mindful that less than a third of the FTSE 100 companies have policies aimed at increasing women's participation in senior management and to challenge the assertion that there are insufficient suitable women (Commission, 2014).

Moreover, corporate culture is twice as important as individual mindsets in determining whether women believe they will succeed (CIPD, 2015). Not only must there be an 'ecosystem' of diversity measures, these must also be supported by a diverse and inclusive culture reflected in leadership styles and performance models (Devillard et al., 2013). Leadership *for* diversity and leadership *with* diversity have been considered across education by Coleman who defines diversity as a concept which:

> encompasses many qualities some of which might be easily visible, for example gender, ethnicity and some religious affiliations and disabilities, and others less visible, for example class or sexual orientation.
>
> (Coleman, 2012b) (p:597)

Both women and men benefit from greater leadership diversity and the healthy diversity of senior teams strengthens the effectiveness of organisations overall. Arguably, creating a culture that is more equitable for women will result in a culture that is fairer for all (Devillard et al., 2013). This is not to say simply that more women at the top will necessarily change the culture for women as there is a danger of equating women in positions of power with feminist women in positions of power. Accordingly, Chapter 6 considers the implications of a critical mass of women at the top in a more nuanced fashion. Nevertheless, apparently there is value to be found for the sustainability of the institution when there is a mix:

> In considering the further question of whether or not having women in senior management impacts on decision-making in HE, it was clear that having both women and men in senior management teams produced better decision-making.
>
> (Bagilhole and White, 2011) (p:196)

Almost six in ten undergraduates are women as are virtually 50 per cent of early career academics (UCU, 2013). Nevertheless, this trend does not extend to more senior roles where recent data identifies that only 21 per cent of professors and 20 per cent of vice chancellors are women; the proportion of male academic staff earning over £50,000 was more than double that of female academic staff; and the median gender pay gap (in favour of men) in the UK was 14 per cent and the mean 19 per cent (ECU, 2014). (Bear in mind when this research was conducted, in 2011, only 13 per cent of vice chancellors were women – 22 altogether as opposed to 35 now.) More generally, the pay gap is still on average 19 per cent (ONS, 2014), giving concern to how long it will be (70 more years according to an International Labour Organisation report marking International Women's Day 2015) before equal pay is achieved. Given it is already 40 years since the equalities legislation, from 2015 the government will make free software available which will enable organisations to calculate their gender pay gap easily and identify issues that may be preventing women from being promoted.

Equality is a cornerstone of higher education philosophy and enlightenment and, as such, it matters that the sector embraces gender equality and is seen to be addressing the missing women conundrum (Jarboe, 2013); not least because not only does higher education contribute billions of pounds to the economy but it also receives equally large sums from public funding bodies which, in turn, must demonstrate that they satisfy equalities legislation (HEFCE, 2013). Moreover, as the missing women at the top of higher education has wider and more serious resonances for women's participation in public life (Warwick, 2004, Morley, 2005) so higher education has a responsibility to model social justice. Consequently, the underrepresentation of women at the top in higher education is a fundamental issue for UK society because:

> Higher education is a pivotal institution in society and the consequences of women's under-representation in positions of authority have wider and more serious resonances for issues of equity and social justice and participation in public life.
>
> (Morley, 1999) (p:4)

As women are predicted to be the majority of all academics by 2020 whereas the same projections show that women will not be fairly represented at professorial level until 2070 at the earliest (Leathwood and Read, 2009), an international grouping of senior women called for gender equality to be made a key performance indicator in quality audits of higher education institutions at the British Council's 'Going Global' conference in 2013. Similarly, at this pace of change it will take 30 years to achieve an equal number of senior women police officers, 45 years to achieve an equal number of women in the senior judiciary, 70 years to achieve an equal number of women directors in FTSE 100 companies and 14 elections to achieve an equal number of women MPs. Ultimately there are 5,400 'missing women' in top jobs across the public and private sectors (Commission, 2011). Thus, higher education is not alone as a sector in which women are underrepresented in senior leadership. Even after 40 years of equality legislation women are hardly visible in positions of power (Coalition, 2013). Across higher education 'the numbers game' has been revealed as a smokescreen masking inherent misogyny (David, 2014; Morley, 2011).

The so-called 'private space' of women and caring for their families, which can be referred to as the gendered division of labour, is often cited as a major reason for this power imbalance. There is a tension here between what may be private choices, practices and responsibilities on the part of women and what actually requires public policy intervention. Many managers still avoid hiring younger women as the cost of maternity leave is too high and women 'aren't as good at their jobs' when they return (The Guardian 12 August 2014). Across higher education research shows that there is a 'motherhood penalty' and a 'fatherhood bonus' for academic careers (Rice, 2014). Without conducive public policy, caring responsibilities will continue to be a barrier to women's (and to some men's) representation at the top. Consequently, much discourse concerns public policy around childcare and broader caring responsibilities given that by equalising labour force participation rates UK GDP could increase 10 per cent by 2030 (McGregor-Smith, 2013).

The need for more women in leadership, so as to create a critical mass, is also a common discourse nowadays (Erkut et al., 2008, Kramer et al., 2006, Klenke, 2011, Osmond, 2009, Zehner and Basch, 2009), and it is possible for this critical mass to challenge entrenched leadership cultures and to offer alternative leadership models and 'protean organisations' (Cabrera, 2009, Eagly and Carli, 2007). This is not to say that all will be well even if a critical mass of women is achieved at the top, for this may not equate with a critical mass of feminist women. Moreover, taking positive action to achieve this critical mass is debated widely (O'Cinneide, 2012). An initial UK government review (Davies, 2011) resisted implementing positive action and instead recommended a target of 40 per cent of boardroom posts being held by women by 2020, with an interim target of 25 per cent by 2015. Although the review fell short of recommending positive action quotas, this being a popular approach taken by some other European countries, it nonetheless implied that quotas would replace targets if progress was not substantial – currently 20.7 per cent with one year to go (Davies,

2014). The Cabinet Office aspired to equal numbers of women and men in permanent secretary level posts and for a short time achieved this target (Hunter, 2011), although the recent return to the status quo suggests that even when a critical mass is achieved the representation of women at the top is fragile and requires persistent positive action.

Political parties are well aware that women's votes count and that women overall are feeling unrepresented at local, regional, national and international levels regardless of their party allegiance. The UK prime minister gave a speech in Brussels in 2012 emphasising the need for a fairer representation of women in all walks of life even though the Conservative Party itself has just 16 per cent of MPs who are women, with Westminster overall managing just 22 per cent women MPs. Only 364 women have ever sat in the House of Commons (7.4 per cent of all persons elected to the House) (Electoral Reform Society, 2014). There is a growing discourse within political circles about adopting positive action to improve the representation of women, despite a Labour MP arguing recently that all-women shortlists have resulted in the feminisation of politics (where women worry about social, educational and family issues rather than international ones). Conversely, both Welsh and Scottish parliaments are losing women and there is concern about why this is happening (Osmond, 2009). The debate about sexism in parliament has been reignited by Harriet Harman who concludes:

> You don't have to openly oppose equality to perpetuate inequality...all it takes is for those in positions of power to do nothing and the status quo prevails. Progress towards equality requires men to change as well as women. Particularly men in positions of power. http://www.theguardian.com/politics/2014/jul/08/harriet-harman-gordon-brown-inequality-labour-sexism.
>
> (Accessed 6 August 2014)

Men in 'positions of power' like the Peer whose alleged sexism has caused controversy for his party during the past ten years. The 'everyday sexism project' is raising awareness of the sexism women encounter in their daily lives, often in higher education and the workplace more generally (Bates, 2014). Research conducted around the world highlighting sexism in higher education made it 'increasingly clear that unconscious bias against women exists' (Times Higher Education, 7 August 2014 about comments by the vice chancellor, Oxford University). This is despite women not being a minority group in the UK population as a whole, although the invisibility of women in public office can make it seem as though they are. Apparently society is ruled by straight, white, middle class, 'default man' (Perry, 2014). Nevertheless, there is a fear that improving the visibility of women will penalise overrepresented groups (such as white, middle-class, able-bodied men) even though the representation of 'minorities' has been found to not only benefit those minorities but also to do so without penalising non-minorities. Thus, representative bureaucracies are more effective than their non- representative counterparts (Meier et al., 1999). Notwithstanding this, positive action may not be ideal as: critical actors may be more important than critical mass; a comprehensive women's movement might be more effective than simple numbers representation; critical mass relies on a false concept of women as monolithic; more feminist legislators of either sex are better than just more women; and more gratuitous women may result in a counterproductive backlash (Etzkowitz et al., 1994).

In summary, only slow progress is being made towards gender equity in higher education leadership and the gender imbalance amongst senior university academics is not simply a UK problem (Davidson and Burke, 2011). Although these disparities exist in other fields as well, the statistics relating to university gender imbalances are particularly concerning, as Davidson and Burke agree, because of the pivotal role that higher education plays in society. Recent research highlights that universities, which should be leading the way in relation to being beacons of good practice, now lag behind every sector except for the judiciary in relation to diversity and equality (Manfredi et al., 2014).

1.2 The genesis of this research study

I returned to full-time education to study for my PhD after a rewarding career in leadership development. Fifteen years ago this career led me into higher education where I worked with academic leaders at all levels, including vice chancellors and pro vice chancellors, across four very different universities. I designed, developed and delivered leadership programmes as well as providing one-to-one support such as mentoring and coaching. Being in such close contact with the academic leadership community allowed me the privilege of experiencing higher education leadership cultures at first hand. Eventually this varied experience stimulated my enquiry about what I perceived at that time as 'the missing women' in academic leadership and I began asking myself the questions 'where are the women?' and 'why are there so few women vice chancellors'?

My experiences in leadership development and my observations around 'the missing women' in leadership led me into exploring gendered leadership cultures and how much higher education leadership cultures were gendered too, so this became a focus of my review of the literature. I realised that in the context of higher education gendered leadership, the concept of organisational culture has been used to refer to a 'complicated fabric of management myths', values and practices that legitimise women's positions at the lower levels of the hierarchy and portray managerial jobs as primarily masculine (Deem, 2003). And that gender is done 'in the symbols, images, rules and values that explicitly and implicitly steer, justify and sometimes question gender distinctions in the organisation' (Benschop and Brouns, 2003) (p:200). The structural, cultural and procedural arrangements of academic organising relate to gender and the emphasis on scientific quality reflects a hegemonic position privileging masculinity (Benschop and Brouns, 2003). So much so that changing women's position in universities requires changes to gendered organisational cultures as well as other kinds of change (O'Connor, 2011). Ultimately:

> Changing men and men's position in universities and their cultures for 'women's place' is defined by men and it is a subordinate one. Men are 'a social category associated with hierarchy and power … management is a social activity that is also clearly based on hierarchy and power … academia is a social institution that is also intimately associated with hierarchy and power'.
>
> (Hearn, 2001) (p:70)

I learned that the interlocked practices and processes that result in continuing inequalities in all work organisations and organisational cultures are inherently gendered (Acker, 2006). Acker refers to 'inequality regimes', and the fact that their creation largely by and for men means that, more often than not, organisational work systems, work practices, norms and definitions reflect masculine experiences, masculine values and men's life situations. Inequality regimes are the intertwined processes and practices that result in systemic inequalities in the workplace. These regimes include norms and assumptions in the work culture that value specific types of work and work processes, define competence and excellence of staff, and shape ideas about the best way to get things done (Meyerson and Kolb, 2000). Leadership in most organisations tends to replicate itself, and in universities, in particular, it operates from a narrow base (Bagilhole and White, 2011). Moreover, gender is not simply imported into the workplace, but itself constructed in part through work whereby it is seen as an organisational accomplishment and leadership cultures are seen as shaping gender identities. Thus, my research study is based upon my interpretation of higher education leadership cultures as both gendered and gendering.

But what is gender and how am I interpreting gender in terms of my enquiry? Although I began my research journey by being concerned with the underrepresentation of women in higher education leadership, my fundamental concern is the performativity of gender in higher education leadership and its implications for the learning of leadership. It is clear that gender, or as Acker has articulated, 'patterned, socially produced, distinctions between female and male, feminine and masculine' (p:250), is a core concept for discerning what is happening with people in their lives at work, and for understanding how people encounter organisations (Acker, 1992).

Gender performativity takes a number of forms which I interpret to mean: that to do gender is to perform it, that to do gender means we have to work at it and that gender is produced through the repetition of gender norms (Holmes, 2007). In terms of my experience of higher education leadership, higher education leaders were 'playing' to their audience and some of my participants talked about this by using what they referred to as 'situational leadership'. In this way we are all actors and, throughout our lives, we alter our behaviour according to how we think others see us: our performances involve gender displays (Goffman, 1979). Correspondingly, the women in my study have worked hard on their gender throughout their career in order to 'fit in' to the prevailing cultures, which demonstrates that gender is a routine that we must work at in everyday interactions (West and Zimmerman, 1987) so much so that:

> We are all constantly working at presenting ourselves as feminine or masculine in relation to others and through this interactive work gender is produced.
>
> (Holmes, 2007) (p:55)

Also, gender is being applied to my research participants by their repetition of gender norms and also by their colleagues who make judgements about these as evidenced by 'she is a token man anyhow' (3). Not only is gender 'done to us', it is socially constructed and a 'stylized repetition of acts' whereby:

> Gender is an identity tenuously constituted in time, instituted in an exterior space through a stylised repetition of acts. The effect of gender is produced through the stylisation of the body and, hence, must

be understood as the mundane way in which bodily gestures, movements, and styles of various kinds create the illusion of an abiding gendered self. This formulation moves the conception of gender off the ground of a substantial model of identity to one that requires a conception of gender as a social temporality.

(Butler and Dawson, 2006) (p:140)

The issue for me when thinking through my study was how much gender mattered in terms of the learning of academic leadership and how much the absence of women academics at the top was attributable to gendered and gendering higher education cultures. Thus, I began to be influenced by sociologists such as Butler and became comfortable with the notion that the creation of gender norms is central to gender practices and also that the many and diverse gender norms are constantly changing and shifting and, therefore, their meaning and our gender can never be fixed. Moreover, gender is not only performed but also performative, and we must attribute a gender to someone to make sense of them as a human being such that:

Only as gendered beings are persons culturally intelligible.

(Butler and Dawson, 2006) (p:16)

Consequently, I found myself asking, with regard to the learning of leadership: how do higher education leaders do gender, how much agency do they have, how does this doing of gender come about and how is this interpreted?

Ultimately, my research project is an emancipatory one in the sense that I am 'situated' in the field of higher education leadership and have an ambition to inform and influence change through gendered leadership cultures whereby more women will be promoted and where there will be greater visibility of women in senior roles. Whether this requires me to be a 'structuralist' (which also requires that I believe my participants and other leaders are structuralists), given my campaign needs people to have a capacity for agency, was an on-going consideration for me. It was clear to me that I was in danger of essentialising or trivialising women by treating the women in my study (and women in higher education leadership generally) as a homogeneous group, which was never my intention.

My understanding of structuralism is that we are shaped into being feminine or masculine by social structures (De Beauvoir et al., 2011). Gender is done to us (and by us) through four main structures namely power, production, emotion and symbolism, which, collectively, create the gender regime that shapes people's lives (Connell, 2002). In contrast, post-structuralism argues that identities are much more complex, fluid and deconstructed such that ultimately there is no category of gender (or women or men for that matter) and there is no such thing as agency with regards to our identity, since everything is determined by the perceptions of others (Derrida, 1976). Post-structuralism has been described as 'the cultural or linguistic turn' where the emphasis on inequalities has been replaced by the exploration of identity and meaning. Post-structuralism does not fix the self, rather the self is positioned in discourse (socially and culturally produced patterns of language) and power is constituted through constructionism (Foucault and Gordon, 1980). Although post-structural feminism recognises that society is gendered, it focuses more on the binary structures that represent masculinity as superior and the extent to which we have agency. Whereas structuralism can see women as victims, it can be argued that post-structuralism reinforces individualism or neo-liberalism. Although post-structuralism acknowledges the fluidity and fragmentation of identity, at the same time it tends to deny that there may be 'a truth' that dictates that dominant discourses are patriarchal.

I found it increasingly problematic to try and label myself regarding my sociological gender position. Was I a structuralist or post-structuralist, a modernist or post-modernist? How much did it matter if I resisted these labels, and what of the tension between realism and relativism? On the one hand, I perceive higher education gendered leadership cultures as 'structural' entities, whilst on the other hand I recognise that, in accordance with post-structuralism, higher education leadership cultures do not exist in themselves, gendered or otherwise, but rather exist in whatever form they take on at any moment in time, being shaped by discourse and text.

Similarly, my feminist epistemology straddles the juxtaposition between structuralism and post-structuralism and acknowledges the value of both in terms of the research project. In the context of post-structuralism I sought to be careful not to see women leaders in higher education as a homogeneous group, nor to generalise their stories and especially not to essentialise womanhood. I accept that intersectionality means that there may be more differences than similarities between women higher education leaders and that the existence of opportunities for some women to become vice chancellors does not necessarily mean equal opportunity for all. Thus:

Black, working-class, gay, and disabled feminists have drawn white, middle-class, able-bodied, heterosexual feminists' attention to the fact that oppressive power relationships are not only dependent on gender, but can occur due to a host of other factors, and can exist between women.

(Francis, 1999) (p:383)

However, feminism for me is a political movement that challenges the status quo, particularly patriarchy, and I have been clear from the outset that I wanted my research to make a difference to gender relations in higher education society [It has been interesting for me to read David's fascinating exploration of feminism, gender and universities as I was proof reading this book and asking myself questions she invited her cohort 2 participants to contemplate (David, 2014)]. In this sense it can be argued that my feminism will never be post-structural as it is based on a 'truth narrative' that patriarchy oppresses women and that this oppression is wrong. In so doing, I chose to use the combined lived experiences of the women in my study as a valid way of knowing (Balbus, 1987), as a means of helping me explore gendered and gendering higher education leadership. This implies that I do not deconstruct the category of woman nor do I avoid the structural inequalities that still exist in higher education. My qualitative approach sits within the feminist tradition of 'prioritising women's own voices in constructing the narrative of their own experiences' (Parsons and Priola, 2013) (p:585). In this way I am taking a modernist or materialist position on feminism which acknowledges that leadership gender identities are being made and done, but which also recognises the structural context of historical gender relations, hegemonic masculinities, as well as the emancipatory nature of my project. As Francis argues:

I conclude, then, that while we may agree theoretically that the self is constituted through discourse, we still feel ourselves to have agency, moral obligation, and preferences for different kinds of discourse; and that creating narratives to structure, or describe our lives, is part of being a human subject. Thus, I still feel that the feminist argument is valid, despite my recognition that it is a modernist grand narrative, based on (probably over-) essentialist generalisations concerning 'males' and 'females'. We can sometimes choose to resist certain discourses and encourage others. I can sometimes recognise when I am being constituted through discourses of gender dualism, and choose whether to draw on alternative discourse to resist such positioning.

Soper (1990) argues that although feminism should move towards indifference feminism and away from difference (essentialist) feminism, we should retain the category 'woman' on the grounds that it is needed to describe and transform women's lives in order to bring us to a position where we can afford to be gender-indifferent.

(Francis, 1999) (p:391)

Within this modernist feminism, I interpret femininities in higher education leadership as 'the other' to masculinities. I propose that leadership in higher education operates through an exchange of masculinities and whilst leaders can and do 'do' femininities (and have them done to them), these are interpreted as 'other' to the masculinities of colleagues through comparison and subordination. This process of 'othering' is familiar to people performing femininities more generally, whether through bodies identified as female or male, because this inequality is at the heart of the feminist movement. Whereas masculinities gender performativity is commonly associated with bodies identified as male, this is not necessarily the case, as explored in this study. Most importantly, masculinities also refer to gender relations and the position of men in the gender order. Masculinity is constructed in relation to what it is not – especially femininity – and we understand what masculinity means by contrasting it to aspects that we consider as being 'not masculine' (Connell, 1995). In addition, hegemonic masculinity represents the pinnacle of masculinity in that the meanings associated with dominant masculinity are those to which all versions of doing masculinity are compared (Connell, 2002).

However, the dominant standard and its meanings change as society changes. Connell (ibid) concludes that although hegemonic masculinity is largely a myth, it is defined against femininity and 'other' identities considered not properly masculine. Similarly, masculinities in higher education leadership are ordinarily associated with male leaders and their leadership styles. Familiar masculinities in leadership include talking more than women in meetings, presenting other people's ideas as their own, showing aggression in the workplace, taking charge and making demands rather than requests, cronyism, standing up and orating, dictating rather than discussing, working long hours, presenteeism, being decisive and tough, prioritising goals and targets, galvanising action and getting results, by whatever means (Buchbinder, 1994, Eagly and Johannesen-Schmidt, 2001).

The importance of the performance and performativity of masculinities for my research is in how I interpret masculinities in higher education leadership in terms of their perpetuation through the learning of leadership. I maintain that certain masculinities are more prevalent in leadership not only because until relatively recently only male bodies frequented the leadership role but also because, inevitably, masculinities signify hegemonic leadership. Hence, people learning leadership within higher education gendered leadership cultures are, by default, learning leadership masculinities regardless of whether they inhabit female or male bodies. Interestingly, my participants interpreted a spectrum of masculinities and positioned their colleagues somewhere within this spectrum such that 'there are more manly men than him' (1). Nevertheless, masculinities themselves change over time and what might have been interpreted as leadership masculinities in higher education when my participants commenced their careers will likely have changed up until the present time. This once again raises the spectre of the structuralist/post-structuralist conundrum insofar as whilst I propose that masculinities are relative, fluid and temporal, I am also mindful that higher education leaders have the agency to adopt masculinities. The lived experience is what my participants present regardless of whether, theoretically, I might want to frame their responses post-structurally. As Francis says:

> It is argued here that despite recent changes in the opportunities available to women, individuals still experience gender as integral to their sense of social identity, and that gender differential behaviour expresses and perpetuates the gender dichotomy which remains deeply entrenched in our psyches.
>
> (Francis, 2002) (p:44)

And that:

> While many people do resist and challenge gender categorisation, the experience can be so traumatic, or liberating, that this resistance itself becomes a dominant cornerstone of that person's sense of identity... this supports the position that the gender dichotomy is a taken-for-granted feature of our society.
>
> (Francis, 2002) (p:43)

As resistance and power are inter-relational then although my research participants are undeniably powerful in their senior role, women do not own power themselves as power is 'everywhere' and 'anywhere' according to Foucault (McNay, 1993). Instead, their power depends upon the intersection between their identities and related discourses. For example, one of the participants might hold power because of her vice chancellor public space but may lose power in her private space as a woman, wife or mother. Equally, her capacity for resistance to the influences of power, and thus her capacity to influence and change things, will be inextricably linked with discourses around her various identities.

Consequently, I interpret power and knowledge as interdependent whilst recognising that there is no 'global truth' of knowledge that will be discovered by my fieldwork. One of the most important features of Foucault's view is that mechanisms of power produce different types of knowledge, which, in turn, bring together 'information' on a person's activities and existence (Foucault and Gordon, 1980); and the knowledge gathered in this way further reinforces exercises of power. Power entails a set of actions performed upon another person's actions and reactions. This post-structural interpretation of power influenced my research study, in particular the methodology and data analysis employed, by making me question both my own interpretation of higher education hierarchy and my perception of the capacity for agency and resistance that women vice chancellors have.

To summarise, the PhD research study featured in this book is underpinned by my position that:

- My research has an emancipatory agenda around making a difference for women in the academy.
- Higher education cultures are gendered and gendering.
- Women (and men) are not a homogeneous group.
- Gender is performative.
- Masculinities (more particularly hegemonic masculinities) are made and done through higher education leadership and the learning of leadership.
- There is a tension between structuralism/post-structuralism and realism/relativism.
- Higher education leadership has a capacity for agency.
- Power and resistance are relational, and power and knowledge are interdependent.
- The lived experiences of senior women leaders are valuable ways of knowing although there is no 'global truth' to be discovered.

1.3 Themes emerging from the research

Three themes emerged during the research project, which are revisited regularly throughout this book. These themes stemmed from a fundamental inquiry into why there are so few women vice chancellors, why the issue is important and why it matters. This book proposes: (i) that women vice chancellors learn leadership through negotiating and navigating gendered leadership cultures, (ii) that these cultures can be interpreted within a theoretical framework which interprets higher education leadership as communities of practice of masculinities and (iii) that having a critical mass of women 'at the top' may help to address these cultures. Hence, the three themes are:

- the negotiation and navigation of higher education gendered leader-ship cultures;
- higher education leadership as communities of practice of masculinities; and
- achieving a 'critical mass' of women at the top.

This thematic analysis accepts that there is an unavoidable tension between my ambition to not essentialise women or interpret higher edu-cation gendered leadership cultures as fixed whilst, at the same time, acknowledges that a data generation method was used that relied on the lived experience of higher education gendered structures.

1.4   Contribution to knowledge

This book represents the culmination of a PhD study which set out to explore the issue of why there are so few women vice chancellors in UK higher education. As such the enquiry itself constitutes a contribution to knowledge, an especially important contribution, and offers a novel perspective on the underrepresentation of women throughout higher education academic leadership because of the way the study frames the voices of women vice chancellors. More specifically, this book makes a significant and important contribution to knowledge by:

- seeking out and engaging with the silent and strange voices of women vice chancellors.

There was a lack of public domain knowledge about the experiences of women vice chancellors within the gendered leadership cultures of higher education. The current cohort of women vice chancellors consti-tutes a group of the first women to have achieved such high office within higher education and, as such, this research is timely and novel. I have been careful not to essentialise women, nor to generalise my findings about this group of women. Nevertheless one aspect of this contribution to knowledge is the insight the data gives to the lived experiences of these pioneering women.

- interpreting higher education gendered leadership cultures, through lived experiences and argument, within my theoretical framework of higher education leadership as communities of practice of masculinities.

I propose that, on the whole, a theoretical framework around higher education leadership as communities of practice of masculinities is valuable for considering why women are under represented in higher education leadership generally and, consequently, why there are so few women vice chancellors. This is a novel framework for interpreting higher education gendered leadership cultures and helps grow knowledge in this field. My contribution has been to take an educational feminist framework and apply it to leadership cultures and the learning of leadership within higher education.

- making the case for positive action across higher education with the aim of achieving a critical mass of women at the top.

This research is novel and significantly important in the way it frames what is happening for women at the top in higher education within the wider context of what is happening for women across all sectors in the UK, within and beyond education. It has been important for me to position my work in this wider context because higher education is a highly influential sector and has the potential to lead change. Throughout the duration of this project there has been a growing national conversation about the 'missing women at the top' to which this research seeks to contribute by looking in-depth at a major sector of the UK economy. Moreover, this research comes from an emancipatory feminism perspective and contributes knowledge to the debate around positive action as a means of bringing about change. Critically, the fundamental issue of social justice is addressed at a time when, as many commentators agree, progress made in the 40 years of equality legislation is faltering and, in fact, slipping backwards (CEDAW, 2013). In summary, I propose that my contribution to knowledge is certainly novel and, given the wider national debate, significantly important.

1.5 The shape of the book

This book has six further chapters followed by references. Chapter 2 explores the higher education gender neutral myth as the foundation for the literature informing my research, whilst Chapter 3 provides information about my research methodology and research participants. The following three chapters consider the data generated by the study through thematic analyses and discussion around the emerging themes introduced in this chapter. Finally, Chapter 7 is about any conclusions to be discovered and a conversation about the way forward. A comprehensive list of references follows.

2
Higher Education: The Gender Neutral Myth

2.1 Background to the literature

More women in senior appointments are important because without a substantial number (some commentators argue at least 30 per cent) women at this level will always seem unusual, odd and strange (McGregor, 2011). This means that women will invariably be remembered for what they are wearing, what they are saying and how they are behaving because of their identity as women, not because of their position. In addition, as the presence of women in numbers is essential for attracting more women to similar roles, 'critical mass' (Kramer et al., 2006) is relevant, although Ely maintains it is women in senior roles that is most critical (Ely, 1995). Bagley, Head of People at Price Waterhouse Coopers, one of three women on a board of 12 executive directors, considers that boosting women within senior levels in an organisation is a key goal because just now only 15 per cent of partners are women despite women making up half of its UK workforce of 10,000 employees. Bagley, also a member of the Opportunity Now advisory board responsible for the 2014 survey of workplace experiences and ambitions of women aged between 28 and 40, comments in the survey press release:

> We know women are confident and ambitious, but they have different goals to men. Until these goals are recognised as different, but valued equally with male priorities, workplaces will continue to disappoint and disillusion all but the most tenacious of women. To make real progress in supporting women's careers, we need workplaces and a society that value women's differences and support these aims. This means getting the basics, such as how people are assessed and rewarded at work, right.

Similarly, Lady Hallett and Lady Jay tabled a debate about the lack of women judges to the House of Lords in November 2011 even though more than 50 per cent of entrants to the law profession are now women. Lady Hale featured on the Today programme on 23 February 2013 arguing for positive action to improve the position for women in the judiciary because 'women have been joining the ranks in even numbers for more than thirty years now' so she believes time alone will not bring change without action. Linklaters, one of the top five commercial law firms making up 'the magic circle', is introducing partnership targets because 'it makes no business sense' for so few women to reach senior positions such that the partnership cannot be 'made up of the best lawyers' (Hobbs, Linklaters Head of Client Sector programme). Even the Bank of England is realising the economic consequences of women's underrepresentation in top jobs: there were no women candidates when the new governor was appointed at the end of 2012. The nine members of the monetary policy committee have always been men until two women were appointed in July 2014, this being similar in the case of the 11 members of the financial policy committee, and their headquarters on Threadneedle Street itself has six governors and 15 other executives amongst which there are five woman (again a significant improvement since the new governor arrived). Thus, the financial world is a very masculine place raising worries about the effect of 'testosterone' levels on the financial trading floors (Coates and Herbert, 2008). Corporate governance of the financial sector has taken priority since the recession of 2008, with examples such as the Cooperative Bank saga, during which its Chairman resigned adding to the discourse about the consequences of unchecked masculinities in the boardroom. Accordingly, the only Iceland bank to survive the crash, Audur Capital, is led by two women with the ambition of incorporating feminine values into finance, and in France the banks with more women at the top have apparently survived better (Ferrary, 2009). Interestingly, for the first time ever women are now leading the US Federal Reserve System, the International Monetary Fund and the German Financial Centre.

As Condoleezza Rice, former US Secretary of State, says 'empowering women isn't just the right thing, it's the necessary thing. And because women are increasingly ruling, the world is changing for the better' (BBC News online viewpoint 8 March 2013 – International Women's Day). So, according to the financial section of *The Guardian* (19 November 2012), 'getting a critical mass of women at the top of major companies will change employment culture for everyone, because what happens to women in management is just a particularly glossy reflection of what happens to women at the other end of the jobs market'. The 30 per cent Club is a group of chairs and chief executive officers (CEOs) committed to improved gender balance at all levels of their organisations through voluntary action (Club, 2010). Their aims in the UK are to achieve a critical mass of 30 per cent women on FTSE 100 boards by the end of 2015 and 30 per cent female representation on executive committees by end of 2017. However, they do not believe mandatory quotas are the best approach, instead aiming for meaningful, sustainable change at all levels. Nevertheless, the recently launched 2 per cent club (a network uniting the 2 per cent of executive and nonexecutive women drawn from the top of the private, public, charity and entrepreneurial sectors and representing all regions of the UK) illustrates the scale of the problem.

The 'critical mass' conversation ultimately leads to controversy about how to make sure more women reach the top, in whatever sector. Davies (2011) shied away from quotas after wide consultation, preferring instead voluntary targets, unlike Norway which introduced quotas ten years ago and now more than 40 per cent of nonexecutive directors in their boardrooms are women. Subsequently, Finland, France, Germany, Iceland, the Netherlands and Spain have all introduced similar legislation (Bertrand et al., 2014). However, this has not been universally applauded, because of the unintended consequences of compulsory measures. Some commentators worry that quotas encourage women to be appointed to meet the targets, not because they are best for the post, and that women quotas simply increase the number of directorships each women holds rather than the number of women *per se*. Nevertheless the introduction of quotas around the world has generated a healthy debate that may lead to the introduction of other measures to improve the gender gap (Dawson et al., 2014). The European Union (EU) recently rejected a proposal to adopt quotas for the representation of women on boards across the EU when tabled by Justice Commissioner Viviane Reding. Although a Commission without a significant number of women is neither 'legitimate nor credible', according to the newly elected president of the European Commission, Jean-Claude Junker, fewer than 10 per cent of women surveyed agree with the introduction of quotas despite almost half of the women respondents having considered that gender has hindered their career or will do in the future (Talent, 2014).

The introduction of quotas has female, as well as male, opponents, for a number of reasons: some women worry that their success will be attributed to them satisfying a legal requirement, rather than being appointed on merit (i.e. women will be promoted beyond their competence); some women deny that there are any barriers to women's success besides the barriers that women create for themselves and some women neoliberalists who make it to the top believing that if they can do it any woman can. Ahrendts, senior Vice President Apple Inc. (and ex-CEO Burberry), dismisses the idea of quotas to boost the number of women in Boardrooms as 'dangerous' despite her being just one of four women CEOs in FTSE 100 companies at the beginning of 2014. Although this is not a position supported by Whittaker (nonexecutive Director at Standard Life and Imperial Oil) who argues that as society has been pursuing this issue for 40 years, and there is still such underrepresentation of women at the top, there will only be true 'equality' when there are as many incompetent women on boards as incompetent men.

Consequently, 'positive action', which means mainstreaming structures, policies and practices through a gender lens, is firmly on the agenda as an alternative to quotas (Bendl and Schmidt, 2013). The Equality and Human Rights Commission (EHRC) report not only highlighted the 'missing women' but also calculated the numbers of years it will take for women to be fairly represented at the current pace of change (Commission, 2011). In higher education it will take at least 70 years for women to be fairly represented in the professoriate, where on average only 21 per cent of professors are women at the moment. Added to which, according to the Chartered Institute of Management (CIM), the average gender pay gap in senior leadership roles in all sectors across the UK is around £10,000 (or £423,000 over a woman's lifetime) and without positive action it will be nearly 100 years before there is parity. Franke, CIM CEO, feels the time has come to tackle this situation more systematically. It will take at least 75 years for pay equality according to the Oxfam International report which urged G20 leaders to tackle gender equality at their meeting in Australia late 2014. Depending on the country context, an extra 20–60 per cent would be added to the GDP of individual G20 countries if the hidden contribution of unpaid work (such as caring for children or carrying out housework) was recognised and valued. Meanwhile, if women's paid employment rates were the same as men's the Eurozone's GDP would increase by 13 per cent (Wakefield, 2014).

Society can often blame underrepresented groups for their position in the social hierarchy so it is not uncommon for women themselves to be blamed for their underrepresentation in leadership (Spar, 2012). Sandberg, Facebook chief operating officer and a woman in her forties with children, reflects that her generation is not going to change the numbers at the top. She blames her women peers for this too, giving three rules (be at the table, never leave until you leave and make your partner a real partner) for women to follow if they are serious about getting on – as though it is that simple and in the gift of women unilaterally to change the status quo, a symptom of contemporary neoliberalism. Recently Sandberg published a book about how women should 'lean in' (rather than holding themselves back, not raising their hands, and lacking self-confidence, hence not 'leaning' in) to organisations regardless of their circumstances (Sandberg, 2013). Often, it appears that if women do not work hard enough to achieve success on their own merit then they have only themselves to blame. Cech and Blair-Loy found that meritocratic explanations tend to be the dominant discourse accounting for differences in the success of women in American culture (Wynn, 2012). They argue that to view her own success as legitimate, a woman has to recognise her own hard work and smart choices as the secrets of her success, which, by implication, blames the lack of success of other women on their failure to do these things. Also, women may not succeed because they do not pay enough attention to planning and developing their careers. It becomes a cycle of neglect, where women's deficits and distractions culminate in their avoidance of mid- and long-term career planning and development, becoming job- rather than career-orientated (Mavin and Bryans, 2002). Women invariably miss out on career development opportunities because they are 'doing the job' rather than 'being in the job' (having a superficial attachment to the role whilst being on the look-out for advancement and promotion) (O'Connor, 2011).

As a result, women-only leadership education is back on the agenda with leading business schools, such as Said at Oxford, launching new leadership education programmes for women. Such education programmes aim to address and challenge, amongst other things, the deficit model, a convenient way to blame women indirectly for their under-representation. The model goes something like this: women are not ambitious enough; women are not confident enough; women are not resilient enough; and so on. It is fair to say that many women struggle with confidence and ambition as Fels says:

> There is something about the idea of ambition that makes women distinctly uncomfortable . . . highly successful women attribute their success to luck and won't admit to being ambitious because they feel it desexualises them and makes them appear self serving and egotistical.

(Fels, 2004) (p:5)

Often my research participants discussed how women's lack of confidence, ambition and resilience were interconnected and how they play out for the underrepresentation of women in leadership:

> For me the clear answer, I think, it is that women don't try as hard as men do putting themselves forward because they are very self reflective, perhaps lack the confidence, and feel knocked back. (13)

Another way, apparently, in which women are responsible for their own downfall is the conflicting demands they place upon their own time. Acker writes about women academics who suffer from three subtle problems, one of which is the conflicting demands of greedy institutions – work and family (Acker and Armenti, 2004). Even if women don't have children themselves, they are prone to be distracted by supporting their students and providing 'departmental housework' which is something that their male colleagues do not do, according to the vice chancellor of Wolverhampton University in her case study on the EHRC website. Pateman sees 'the woman's problem' from another perspective by arguing that masculine work habits within gendered leadership cultures are still the norm at senior levels so much so that leaders will have a 'wife' who holds responsibility for the private domain so that men can devote themselves to public, organisational life (Pateman, 1988). This certainly featured in my data with at least one of the participants having sympathy with the proposition that 'what women vice chancellors really need is a wife'.

From this review of the background to the literature I conclude in sympathy with Morley (2013) that there are three approaches which together can address the 'missing women' in leadership namely paying attention to the structural issues within institutions (fixing the organisation), paying attention to gendered ways of knowing (fixing the knowledge) and paying attention to women themselves (fixing the women). The remainder of this chapter reviews the literature through the lens of these three approaches.

2.2   The negotiation and navigation of higher education gendered leadership cultures: *Fixing the organisation*

2.2.1   Exposing the gender neutral myth

Studies within the gendered organisation field emerged because feminist scholars revisited organisation theory and research so that women's experiences and voices could be represented (Calas and Smircich, 1992,

Ford et al., 2008, Martin and Collinson, 2002). I propose, along with Gherardi, that it is only 'common sense' that any organisational culture is 'strongly gendered' because organisations themselves are gendered (Gherardi, 1995). Moreover, rather than organisational cultures reacting and responding to the gendered nature of the world outside, organisational cultures have a greater impact (Wicks and Bradshaw, 2002). In other words, gendered organisational cultures contribute to the gendering of society and the shaping of identities beyond the public space. So being gender neutral is impossible and accepting gendered organisational cultures as inevitable fails to recognise that:

> Organisations are cultures, places and spaces for contested meanings, rather than manipulable accessories, even instruments to performance. Changes in organisational cultures are possible, therefore, through the renewed social construction of gender in work-life localities.
>
> (Aaltio et al., 2002) (p:78)

And that:

> The specific behaviours and values that women and men are rewarded for showing, how organisations themselves socialise women and men differently, and thus help shape gender identities in society at large.
>
> (Aaltio et al., 2002) (p:138)

Organisational culture is defined 'as something an organisation has, something an organisation is, and something an organisation does' (Bagilhole, 2007), with Tierney suggesting that it 'derives its force from the values, processes and goals held by those most intimately involved in the organisation's workings' such that:

> An organisation's culture is reflected in what is done, how it is done, and who is involved in doing it. It concerns decisions, actions and communication both on an instrumental and a symbolic level.
>
> (Tierney, 1988) (p:3)

Thus, although universities present themselves as gender neutral meritocracies, concerned with the creation and transmission of scientific, objective knowledge, they are instead gendered organisations because:

As staff bring their personal interests into organisations and that these shape the way they discharge their functions, we must also accept that gendered perceptions, practices and attitudes will be present too.

(O'Connor, 2011) (p:172)

Universities, like all organisations, are made up of people, the staff and students of the institution. These people will perform their gender at work just as they do in everyday life outside of work. In this way, an institution becomes a microcosm of society. People do not leave their gender identities at the door when they enter the workplace. Instead, people continually make and do their identities in the workplace, in the home and at leisure. So gender is in continual production in universities and in the leadership of universities. Gender is produced and reproduced in the positioning, judgements and relations that occur on a daily and consistent basis. In this way it is inconceivable for universities to be gender neutral. Thus, higher education institutions like all other institutions are gendered and gendering. This realisation, in part, formed the genesis of my study because during my ten years working in leadership development in higher education I came to see men, or rather masculinities, as making and doing legitimate senior leadership across the sector.

The relatively recent opening up of higher education to women means that men, and the power of men, predominates and that men's ways of performing masculinities prevail. The way universities operate, through their structures, processes and practices, reinforces these masculinities. Acker argues that formal practices and policies construct divisions along gender lines (both vertically and horizontally) with men in a majority in the most powerful positions (Acker, 1992). She says 'gender is implicated in the fundamental ongoing processes of creating and conceptualising social structures' (p:147). In other words, gendering is in 'the marrow of organisation process' (Knights and Murray, 1994) (p:xiv) which is a reflection upon the social micro processes through which masculine power is promulgated, maintained and resisted.

So it is in sympathy with my interpretation of feminism that organisations are gendered and gendering. We make knowledge together in organisations and that knowledge is inevitably gendered because of how the inevitable organisational politics reflects gender politics in society (Spender, 1981). Organisations are being made and done all the time, there is no fixed organisation state, which is why Mackenzie

Davey explores women's accounts of organisational politics as gendering processes:

> Organisational political processes are seen as fundamental to gender in organisations: first because political activity is seen as gendered and masculine and contrary to female identity; secondly because politics is part of the informal system which constructs organisations from which outsiders are excluded; and finally because political activity is linked to the performance, achievement and maintenance of power.
>
> (Mackenzie Davey, 2008) (p:650)

Consequently, the women Mackenzie Davey interviewed presented a persistent construction of organisational politics as masculine and inconsistent with their identity as a woman. Thereby women and femininities are excluded from the work of organisational politics and, despite their presence in large numbers, are still largely invisible as far as power, influence and institutional gendering is concerned.

Acceptable leadership, the enabler of successor leaders and hence the learning of leadership, is defined by maleness. The way we talk about leadership using male and masculine language and constructs in itself helps to define acceptable (and conversely less acceptable) leadership (Wajcman, 1998). The masculine military language adopted by leadership excludes women; even the public voice of women is mainly silent, and therefore strange (Beard, 2014). Also, women's monitoring of their language as a survival strategy may also make their voice harder to hear (Baxter, 2011). Leaders practising alternative styles can become subject to the process of 'othering' (Butler and Dawson, 2006) whereby they divert from mainstream (malestream) behaviours and become recognised as 'the other', always on the outside of the leadership community and practising 'legitimate peripheral participation' (Wenger, 1998).

Moreover, most organisations are presented as fundamentally rational entities and this helps to create their masculine identity. Femininity is not, and has never been, associated with rationality (De Beauvoir et al., 2011), and masculinity suggests rationality whereas femininity suggests emotionality instead. Ford concerns herself with the making and doing of our organisational identities and similarly argues that there is such a thing as an 'ideal employee' who is rational and disembodied so:

> Organisational structures, cultures, and everyday practices have all been shown to constitute the 'ideal employee' and especially the

ideal manager as a disembodied and rational figure, one which fits more closely with the cultural images of masculinity rather than femininity. Femininity on the other hand has tended to be associated with embodiment, emotions and sexuality; as such it is constituted as subordinate to 'male' rationality and possibly out of place in rational organisations.

(Ford et al., 2008) (p:81)

My experience of higher education, both as a leadership development professional and as a researcher, means that I am familiar with this presentation of universities as rational, gender neutral organisations, where disembodied workers thrive. It is almost as though the liberal culture (and more recently neoliberalism) of higher education encourages this interpretation of the sector as one where all people are the same and gender is irrelevant. This is the myth of the gender neutral culture because gender constructs higher education in so many ways. For example, Acker favours the term 'disembodied worker' to describe ambitious women who by their very nature are as flexible about work and their working lives as their rational male counterparts (Acker, 1992). Because gender is performative, it is constantly being done by us and to us whether in the workplace or outside. Similarly, everywhere is a 'site of gender construction' (Alvesson and Due Billing, 2009) (p:119), the workplace no more or less so. And I am in sympathy with poststructuralism here because:

Post structural feminist thinking throws a challenge to the concept of the unified and coherent individual of western philosophical tradition of the disembodied subject governed by conscious and rational thought. Instead, it seeks to deconstruct hegemonic assumptions of whole and coherent subjects with a unified sense of identity, and to draw attention to the shifting, complex and at times contradictory subject positions and the plurality of subjectivities.

(Ford et al., 2008) (p:78)

Needless to say, as a double bind, women discover throughout organisational politics that organisations are in fact highly emotional and irrational, this being charged by the emotions, rather than the rationality, of masculinities. Such masculine emotionality within organisations is demonstrated through performances like game playing, back stabbing and ingratiation. So much so that game playing, back stabbing and other such activities are men's emotional work (Mackenzie Davey, 2008). This is why gendered organisational cultures and gendering leadership practices are unfair, not just to the many women who are the focus of this study but also to many men. Those people (women and men) who perform gender through femininities and 'alternative' masculinities will be marginalised by the emotional, rather than the rational, work of organisations so that gendered organisational cultures and the gendering of organisations penalises anything other than mainstream (malestream) masculinities. Although many men do not fit in either, so gendered culture is not just about masculinities it is about a certain kind of masculinity, the hegemonic kind (those with the predominant influence as a group over others) and:

> While women in this study explicitly suffered from gendered organisational politics we might expect it to be linked to a specific kind of masculinity or indeed to the processes by which any elite group maintains power.
>
> (Mackenzie Davey, 2008) (p:667)

Thus, contrary to higher education being gender neutral, it is perpetuating a culture wherein gender is actually made because:

> Gender is not simply imported into the workplace: gender itself is constructed in part through work. Gender is thus partly seen as an organizational accomplishment... workplace culture is seen as constructing beliefs about and self-understandings of men and women, what is masculine and feminine, thus shaping gender identities. Organisations can be seen as sites of gender construction.
>
> (Alvesson, 2002) (p:119)

These sites of gender construction inevitably have rules of engagement and there are many ways in which the supposed gender neutral organisational rules discriminate against women, femininities and alternative masculinities. For example, the emphasis on high quality research papers, international conferences, full-time employment and the general valorisation of the lone academic worker all contribute to only 21 per cent of professors being women and the discrepancy between the average age of women reaching vice chancellor level and the average age of their male counterparts. More importantly, what really matters is the way in which gendered structures, processes and practices are presented as gender neutral whereas they actually perpetuate inequalities (Van den Brink, 2012, Van den Brink, 2009). Added to which, often the literature on organisational development and management practice fails to question its gendered nature and instead pervasive associations between men, power and authority are taken for granted so:

> The potential harm they have on both women and men stems from the way in which these rules are presented and interpreted as gender neutral, taken for granted, and institutionalised, when in fact they serve to maintain sex inequalities that disadvantage women.
> (Prasad, 1997) cited in (Wicks and Bradshaw, 2002) (p:208)

These sex inequalities can lead to what Morley calls 'misrecognition' which relates to the power relations that 'bestow or withhold relevant status and rewards differentially on members of different groups' (Morley, 2011). It is my interpretation that misrecognition is also another contraindication of the gender neutral institution. I maintain that women's work in academia is often misrecognised leading to their pay differentials, lack of promotion and delayed career progression. Many of my participants are concerning themselves with these inequities in their own institutions and beginning to look more closely at what is actually happening to pay and reward through a gender lens, this being discussed more fully in the data analysis chapters. It is significant that Higher Education Funding Council (HEFCE), Higher Education Statistics Agency (HESA), Equality Challenge Unit (ECU), University and College Employers Association (UCEA) and Committee of University Chairs (CUC) are now working together to profile their ambition for gender equality in an attempt to influence higher education institutions to act, and to act now (Ross and Schneider, 2014).

Moreover, whilst neoliberalism seems to deny the masculinity of higher education gendered leadership cultures, at the same time there is a discourse emerging about the 'feminisation' of the sector now that there has been a rise in the visibility of women. The number of women in higher education has risen throughout this century – as students, as teaching staff, as middle managers and as leaders – and this visibility has contributed to a rising panic about whether the culture in the sector is becoming feminised (Yakaboski, 2011). This discourse around a feminised culture has been accompanied by an outcry, or moral panic, about the danger that this feminisation brings to higher education and what should be done about it (Leathwood and Read, 2009). In contrast, much evidence confirms that higher education and its institutions – through their websites, symbols, buildings, business processes, leadership and images – continue to demonstrate masculinities which are most definitely not gender neutral (Leathwood and Read, 2009). Women might be entering the elite professions and social spaces but the senior positions appear to remain resistant to feminisation. Morley confirms this in her work on higher education around the world and uses the professions of higher education and medicine as examples (Morley, 2011). In other words, just as Lady Hallett has concerns about the underrepresentation of women in the judiciary despite many years of women entering the legal profession in greater numbers than men, so higher education seems resistant to women reaching the top in representative numbers despite the so-called 'feminisation' of the sector.

I am particularly interested in this feminisation argument and found my research participants to be too. I can see that there are many more women in the middle ranks in universities and especially in administration. Invariably when I facilitated leadership development events there was a preponderance of women on 'management' events' but a complete dearth of women on 'leadership' ones. Added to which, women in administration regularly voiced their feelings of inferiority to their academic colleagues so if the bulk of the increasing numbers of women are in administration then feminisation certainly does not equate with power and influence.

Thus, given that higher education is definitely not gender neutral, whose university is it anyway (Wagner et al., 2008)? Wagner's research is based on essays about what life is like for 'minorities' (in which she includes women) in a Canadian university in an attempt to see whether the equality policies of the past 25 years have actually made a difference. I am as disappointed as Wagner with the findings that gender runs throughout these essays like letters in a stick of rock and have come to a similar realisation that women (and other underrepresented groups) are marginalised and that universities 'belong to' white, middle-class, heterosexuals (Pringle, 2008). In an attempt to overcome this, a woman vice chancellor has commissioned more than 50 portraits of women to be displayed on the walls of the institution.

In summary, in this section I have explored and argued my position that far from being gender neutral universities are in fact highly gendered and gendering. So much so that as a woman vice chancellor in Western Australia says during case study research involving her:

> In effect the customary examples, languages and concepts that evoke leadership associate organisational power with men, and leadership with masculinised ways of knowing (such as tough-mindedness, emotional detachment) and doing (such as assertive self-promotion, making 'hard' decisions and disconnection from family responsibilities). The forces, intensities and desires gendering

this woman vice chancellor disguise heroic masculinity as gender-neutrality.

(Eveline, 2005) (p:656)

2.2.2 Managerialism

Reinforcing this 'heroic masculinity' is the professional 'man'ager and masculine identity work (Barry et al., 2003) which underpins the ongoing and burgeoning trend of higher education in this neoliberal age as a business rather than a social good. Alongside this trend, as I have argued above, the visibility of women in higher education has come about partly because of the rise of 'new managerialism' which refers to the growing middle ranks of academic managers, many of whom are women. This visibility is not necessarily positive and helpful to the cause of women's career development (Deem, 2007, Bagilhole and White, 2013). Instead these roles dilute the underrepresentation statistics, deflecting attention away from the scale of the problem. At the same, time new managerialism jobs are another level of bureaucracy, with never-ending administrative deadlines, normally involving lots of responsibility but very little authority so:

> Feminisation of an occupation is not tantamount to evidence that women have achieved equality with men or that women have successfully wrestled jobs from men. Rather feminisation points to the intersection of economic and social changes which position women in particular kinds of work. Traditionally, feminisation has been understood as the replacement of relatively expensive male workers with less expensive female workers as work has been redesigned and codified. Thus the feminisation of management is not simply about more women reaching management posts. Management posts themselves have changed too with the codification of management practices and the greater combination of management with other work and the delegation of its functions to lower levels of the organisation.
>
> (Deem et al., 2000) (p:233)

Deem first studied further education at the turn of the century when the sector had transitioned into Incorporation, when colleges were taken out of local authority control. In 2007 she studied the impact of new managerialism on higher education. Also increasingly, universities have transformed from communities of scholars to 'workplaces' and have adopted new public management ideology promoting a more business-focused approach. She reflects upon the impact of this transformation on women arguing that, yes, there are many more women but every-one, both women and men, have been coerced into the target-driven culture where less attention is paid to the real needs of students and staff. McNay also writes about 'from the collegial academy to corpo-rate enterprise' and the imposing gendering of managerialised cultures (McNay, 1995). I agree that although it is clear that there are many more women in positions of middle management, these women are not in powerful leadership roles which influence the gendered and gendering cultures. Instead, large numbers of women in the middle management fuel gendered leadership cultures because management itself becomes a form of corporate housekeeping rather than a decision making and influencing activity. Ultimately, women in lower middle management roles may find themselves with 'a foot in the revolving door' of leader-ship, not necessarily on the ladder to more senior leadership positions and even becoming resistant to these owing to the nature of the work (Acker, 2014).

It is not just in higher education where new managerialism and restructuring of middle management is taking place. In further educa-tion the trend has already happened and the feminisation of middle management is a key part of restructuring itself. Pritchard (2010) talks about the remasculinisation of further education management, with women's previous outsider positioning enabling them to be recruited to middle manager posts, bringing with this a highly problematic loyalty to the commercial ethos of corporate colleges. To this extent, women are victims of another double bind, similar to the myth of rational organisa-tions: in order to undertake their management job well they have to sign up to commercial masculinities, thereby perpetuating gendered organi-sational cultures. There is no suggestion that organisations are changing to embrace women, but, rather, women must change to embrace mas-culine cultures. Women's experiences of leadership in this managerialist culture are not necessarily positive and even bring about their own resis-tance to traditional promotional career routes as their attractiveness wanes (O'Connor et al., 2014). It is apparent that new managerialism brings about 'women in men's clothing' or little more than 'lipstick on the gorilla', the title of Saunderson's work on this. Saunderson explored how the new managerialism of institutional structures and processes impact upon academic women's identity structures and processes. She argues that the continuing valorisation of equality policies without their assimilation into the core institutional culture will lead to little more than 'lipstick on the gorilla' (Saunderson, 2002). This is espe-cially relevant to the 'operates as a boundary' element of my theoretical framework around leadership communities of practice of masculinities which I explore more fully in the next section.

Ultimately the association of tasks such as finance, selling and premises with masculinity both utilises gender and has gendered consequences. In addition, the increasing focus on performance evaluation creates new work identities and the understanding of professionalism, as educational organisations reorganise their responsibilities, functions and priorities and:

> This climate puts pressure on emerging leaders in universities. In terms of career progression, women may be more vulnerable than men to potential deleterious effects of this new culture.
>
> (Airini et al., 2011) (p:46)

Bureaucracy itself can disadvantage women (Ferguson, 1984) because people working in a bureaucracy have to learn the skills necessary to cope with subordinate status, just as women invariably have always learned as part of being 'the second sex or other' (De Beauvoir et al., 2011). Now that the academic environment is characterised by different forms of 'specific masculinities' and by more general masculine criteria imported from the corporate world, how do women leaders in academia address the management of change in the context of this new corporate managerialism (Hearn, 2001, Brooks and Mackinnon, 2001)? Diversity in leadership, and the impact this corporate managerialism culture change has had upon the diversity of senior leadership roles, has been revisited by the Leadership Foundation for Higher Education (LFHE) partly through a round-table exercise (Bebbington, 2012) which culminated in a research project into the career trajectories of the alumni of their top management programme (Manfredi et al., 2014). This research highlights how far fewer women on these programmes have been promoted compared with their male peers.

Alongside the managerialism of the sector is the ongoing cultural trend in higher education of the audit culture which impacts unfairly on women academic leaders (Morley, 2003). Audit culture involves structures and processes of masculinities such as 'quantitative' analysis methods, statistics, measuring things that can be observed, the creation of 'experts', the production of 'hard evidence' and its own audit discourse. Morley also argues that there is evidence to suggest that teaching quality is female dominated and research quality is male dominated, prompting her to suggest there is a morality of quality with women heavily responsible for student-focused services. I maintain that performances seemingly appropriate for this audit culture reflect images of masculinity, such as rationality, measurement, objectivity, control and competitiveness. In general, although somewhat essentialist, men are the natural inhabitants of this audit organisational life and women are out of place in these organisational cultures (Gherardi, 1995).

Ultimately, new managerialism reinforced by rampant neoliberal cultures means that, women are now facing both 'glass ceilings' which prevent them from realising their aspirations and 'glass walls' which restrict their earnings and prevent them from reaching the operational roles at the heart of institutions. Although that is not to say that women want to turn the clock back either. Women academics:

> May have reservations about the new cultures of higher education but they are not necessarily nostalgic for times past. They are very aware of the shortcomings of former systems in which ... barriers to progress are drawn along gendered lines.
>
> (Bagilhole and White, 2011) (p:150)

On the whole, I maintain that higher education senior leadership is more available to those academics who not only 'fit' well with 'new managerialism, audit processes and structures' (and austerity measures) but also to those who engage with prevailing discourses, namely those endorsed by higher education leadership communities of practice of masculinities.

2.3   Higher education leadership as communities of practice of masculinities: *'Fixing the knowledge'*

The foregoing literature review makes reference to the 'rational' organisation and how that organisation therefore generates 'masculinities', since rationality is always associated with the masculine and male. So the history of reason is the history of the gendered metaphor (Wajcman, 1998) with men being synonymous with reason and women with non-reason. The construction of women as 'other' not only affects the disrespect that some people have for women, it also affects the tasks women are given and the expectations women themselves, as well as men, have of women. Regardless of the vastly increasing numbers of women in the academy – as students, early career academics, administrative, clerical and junior/middle managers – there is considerable evidence that women are still 'other' within the academy. Hence the relevance of Simone De Beauvoir's statement:

Humanity is male and man defines woman not in herself but as relative to him; she is not regarded as an autonomous being...she is simply what man decrees...she is defined and differentiated with reference to man and not he with reference to her; she is incidental, the inessential as opposed to the essential. He is the Subject, he is the Absolute – she the other.

(De Beauvoir et al., 2011) (p:18)

Why does it matter then that women, as 'the other', are underrepresented in higher education senior leadership and what do we mean by representation anyway? Will a truly democratic organisation require representation of all of its constituent members? Although women are not a minority group (nor a homogeneous one), nevertheless, women (in all their guises) come from a position of 'the other' and so appear as though they are a minority group. With regard to representation, it is the diversity of membership that matters rather than percentages of difference. Higher education senior leadership communities are seriously lacking in diversity overall. Mostly, they comprise white, middle-aged, able-bodied, seemingly heterosexual, middle-class men. According to Rice, there can only be three reasons for this (women aren't good enough, women don't want to do it, and something structural is happening to disadvantage women) and for him quite obviously it is structural (Rice, 2014). Women's representation amongst these communities is essential because not only will more women change the landscape for all women, it will also bring diversity to leadership communities and their decision making, thereby making organisational culture more inclusive and of benefit to all. This is not to say that more women necessarily means more feminist women and I discuss the more nuanced critical mass debate later. Nevertheless, the rise in the size of the female student population, as a larger percentage of a much larger proportion overall of young people moving through to higher education, has attracted much media comment. Apparently, the current trend is more about the 'failure' of men than the 'success' of women and this failure is being portrayed as a social concern. Rather than celebrating women's achievements, such discussion centres on young men being emasculated. Society worries about the rising profile of young women in higher education in a way that it has never worried about a similar preponderance of men (Leathwood and Read, 2009). This panic about the success of 'the other' exacerbates that discussed above about the feminisation of higher education overall and therefore the feminisation of higher education debate (Leathwood and Read, 2009, Morley, 2011) can be interpreted as a fear of 'the other'.

Simply, feminisation can be seen as a type of chaos, or of things being out of place with the dominant group being seen as the 'rational and reasonable gatekeepers of due social order' and guardian of what is appropriate. Like an authority figure claiming that 'enough is enough':

> One of the most dangerous aspects of the feminisation hysteria, in my view, is that it silences advocacy for gender equality and re-positions women as problematic subordinates.
>
> (Morley, 2011) (p:227)

And:

> The feminisation discourse implies that a woman's place is in the self-minimising minority. If they dare to fight their way out of that role, they are conceptualised as a threat to social cohesion.
>
> (Morley, 2011) (p:229)

Hence, leadership concerns 'doing gender' (Wharton, 2005) in which women are in a lose-lose situation. In heroic leadership times (when an individual leader was presumed to save the organisation so being a 'hero'), women doing gender will invariably fail to meet the organisation's expectations because many women do not operate in this way. In post heroic leadership times (when collaboration and cooperation prevail) women doing gender will result in women being more inclined to possess the required skills and behaviour (Skeggs, 2004). Because of the 'practice as a source of coherence' element of my theoretical framework around higher education leadership communities of practice of masculinities, why it is that gender as performed by a male member of staff is interpreted differently to that performed by a female staff member? For example, university leaders are familiar with men performing masculinities, and in fact expect and reward this behaviour. However, when women 'play the game' and try to fit in by behaving similarly, there is a mismatch of expectations which can lead to uncertainty, suspicion and unpopularity. In the end women find themselves in a culture full of contradictions. So:

> When a woman behaves as a leader and exercises authority, it implicitly suggests that women's leadership performance 'fits' and fits in. This obliges women to play a range of roles depending on the

circumstances. Fundamentally women are a threat to the worldview of their male colleagues and must 'play the game' and 'learn the rules', that is, conform to the male worldview, accept their (limited) role, or to be excluded for transgressing these boundaries.

(Fitzgerald, 2013) (p:7)

This effort of 'fitting in' positions ambitious women in a double bind whereby masculine models of leadership are out of reach (Catalyst, 2007, Francis, 2010). Performing femininities excludes women from 'the boys club' yet performing as 'one of the boys' is frowned upon (Acker, 2010, Eveline, 2005). Thus, invariably, leadership roles become 'undoable' jobs for women (Chesterman et al., 2005). As they see around them masculinities being rewarded much more than femininities, they then perform similarly but find they are not accorded the same levels of respect (Bagilhole, 2007). Indeed, successful women overall are often accredited with doing masculinities in a feminine way, basically 'putting lipstick on the gorilla' (Saunderson, 2002). Given that the literature suggests this experience is common at all levels of the academy, it would appear that these communities of practice of masculinities influence the prospective careers of academics across the sector from the outset.

In Priola's study, the participants were women leaders on a business school management team who were 'being female, doing gender' and described leadership femininities and masculinities from their lived experiences. Despite the high concentration of women managers in their leadership team, this did not have an impact on the gender dimension of the institution because:

On the whole, while a certain level of support and care has been recognised by the participants, the school does not show a feminine orientation. Expressing emotions is perceived as weak and negative...the academic managers at this institution present themselves as supportive and thoughtful but efficient rational and firm. To some members of staff, the top management team appears considerate but bureaucratic, goal driven, controlling and distant. The suggestions that the dean may be unpredictable and that one needs to 'keep the guard up' may also give an insight into the contrasting and contesting identity work of someone who may want to be caring and supportive but is afraid of losing the control and authority over people.

(Priola, 2007) (p:33)

However, it should be noted that this was within the context of the rest of the university still having predominantly male leaders and the business school having to fit into the established leadership cultures of masculinities. Nevertheless, this example illustrates well my 'higher education leadership as communities of practice of masculinities' framework because the gender of leaders is not especially relevant but, rather, it is the prevailing leadership culture of masculinities which requires members of leadership communities to make and do a shared repertoire. Similarly, Pritchard found that the women in her study considered themselves to be:

> Less strategic than males in managing their careers and more submissive to authority; they thought that they themselves needed to behave in the same way as men to succeed; and that men had historically and contemporaneously dominated their subject.
>
> (Pritchard, 2010) (p:18)

Doing gender in the workplace means appreciating that there are masculine and feminine interpretations to doing job roles, interpersonal relationships and organisational culture. Doing gender suggests that leadership genders are being done by us and to us (Butler, 2006), that masculinities are not necessarily done by men in the workplace and can sometimes be done by women. Masculinities are invariably more powerful in leadership terms and the interpretation of gender for powerful people. Unsurprisingly, this translates into an unequal representation of men in powerful positions in universities so much so that:

> The rationale then for wanting to see a substantially increased number of women in positions of power and influence in the academy is ultimately about the legitimation of a gender perspective in a university's work and about ensuring that curricula and research programmes across the system are not purely male constructs.
>
> (Brown, 2004) (p:13)

Demonstrating femininities on the other hand can be labelled as practising 'soft skills'. These skills include behaviours such as listening to and supporting our colleagues and students, taking time to solve problems thoroughly rather than quickly and visibly, caring about our team's well-being, giving our time willingly for the benefit of others, working above and beyond our contract to make sure things run smoothly, collaborating with colleagues, showing concern for others' difficulties in the job, being available when needed, even unannounced and at times inconvenient to our own workload (Machado-Taylor and White, 2014). In leadership terms 'soft' means embracing a transformational leadership style which research shows contrary to being soft, actually produces more sustainable organisations in the long term (Alimo-Metcalfe, 2005). This is discussed more roundly by Eagly et al. (2001) when they consider the impact of gender on transformational, transactional and laissez faire leadership styles, and argue that masculinity in the workplace is respected for its no-nonsense approach and timeframed objectives. In universities, this emphasis on masculinities may mean that many men are alienated and excluded from leadership roles too, given that men may choose academia as a career because of its liberalism and reputation for freedom of expression (Letherby, 2001).

Haake found, in accordance with Foucaultian thinking, that the power relations of discourse make it possible for women, but not men, to talk about gender and academic leadership as being connected to each other. She interviewed women and men heads of department at the beginning of their period of office and after four years in post. At the beginning there was no reference by the women or the men to gender in their role but after four years all the women's identities were gender driven, meaning being a woman was as fundamental to their professional identity as being a leader (Haake, 2009). The implication here for my study connects with the gender neutral agenda that I explored above. Those people, more often than not men, who belonged to and held full membership of leadership communities of practice of masculinities, invariably did not notice the lack of diversity in their community and, most likely, never saw the effectiveness of their community as being compromised by this lack of diversity and underrepresentation of other groups. Recent wider research also confirms that women in the workplace see gender as a barrier in a way men do not (Morrissey and Nawrockyi, 2014). This position is reinforced by O'Connor's findings in her study of leadership across the eight universities in Ireland where men were much more likely to deny the gendered leadership cultures there (O'Connor, 2011).

Ultimately, this lack of leadership diversity combined with the gender neutral myth of higher education means that women are disadvantaged and disorientated within leadership communities of practice of masculinities. Often women doing leadership means many women face a contradiction between their identities that arise from societal roles and contexts facing women in business and management, with the specific career and work-life issues of women in these fields, organisational processes affecting women and the role of women as leaders in business and management. When commenting on 'doing gender' in the workplace, Bilimoria sums up the dilemma that women face:

> One feature of women's situation that is not shared by men is that their gender role and leadership roles are usually not consistent in the qualities that they emphasise. Because of this incongruity between the primarily communal qualities that people associate with women and the primarily agentic qualities that people associate with successful leaders (and with men) women face cross-pressures. If they conform to their gender roles, they can seem too feminine to be a good leader. If they conform to their leader role, they can seem too masculine to be a good exemplar of womanhood. The norms associated with the female gender roles allow people to tolerate harsh, controlling competitive behaviours from men more than from women. Indeed people may to some extent expect such behaviours in men but sanction women for similar behaviours.
>
> (Bilimoria and Piderit, 2007) (p:287)

2.3.1   Communities of practice

I came to my research 'situated' in higher education leadership development work that involved me mixing with senior leaders in a variety of forums both as a leadership development practitioner and in my role as head of a corporate service. Over time, I became fascinated by the underrepresentation of women in leadership, from professor to head of department/school to dean of faculty to pro vice chancellor and through to vice chancellor level. I was equally fascinated by the lack of attention that this underrepresentation received and how little it was ever mentioned. In my work with groups of senior leaders in a number of settings (one-to-one meetings, coaching/mentoring sessions, small group meetings, action learning groups, group training events, conferences, and senior management team forums), I witnessed a prevailing leadership culture of masculinities that appeared to be both unchallenged and unchallengeable. This experience has formed the genesis of my research project and as such I began evaluating theoretical frameworks that might help me explore my own lived experiences.

From my review of the published literature and my research into the 'missing women' in higher education leadership, I wondered whether the informal organisational learning group, a 'community of practice', might provide a plausible working theoretical framework for my study. Taking senior academic leadership as a whole, the prerequisites of a community of practice are satisfied – domain of knowledge, community of people and shared practice. Through participation in the community its members establish norms and build collaborative relationships. Their interactions as members create a shared understanding of what brings them together, their joint enterprise. As part of its practice the community produces a set of communal resources, their shared repertoire, and these can include both literal and symbolic meanings such as dress, speech and behaviour. These collaborative relationships are the ties that bind the members of the community together as a social entity. A community of practice is not merely a club of friends or a network of connections between people. Rather it has an identity defined by a shared domain of interest. In pursuing their interest in their domain, members engage in joint activities and discussions, help each other and share information (Wenger, 1998). Interacting and learning together are prerequisites for communities of practice, although members do not necessarily work together on a daily basis. Members of a community of practice are by definition practitioners who develop a shared repertoire of resources (such as experiences, stories, tools) and thereby develop shared practice. Communities of practice provide a context for a group of people to learn new skills, knowledge, behaviours and attitudes. Arguably people belong to a number of communities of practice all the time, some voluntarily and enthusiastically and some not so willingly (and their development of a shared practice may be less conscious) and these communities of practice exist in both public and private spaces – home and family, as well as work and leisure for example.

Originally, communities of practice were rooted in sociocultural theory, based on the proposition that learning is a group phenomenon and evidence of people learning in groups (or communities of practice) in the workplace became the foundation for organisational learning, stretching the concept of individual learning beyond the interpersonal boundary into organisational culture (Senge, 1990). Senge expanded these theories into the 'learning organisation' which presupposed that communities of practice are first and foremost about harnessing its members' performance. It was in this context that Lave and Wenger first defined communities of practice as:

> A set of relations among persons, activity and world, over time and in relation with other tangential and overlapping communities of practice. A community of practice is an intrinsic condition for the existence of knowledge, not least because it provides the interpretive

support necessary for making sense of its heritage. Thus participation in the cultural practice in which any knowledge exists is an epistemological principle of learning. The social structure of this practice, its power relations, and its condition for legitimacy define possibilities for learning.

(Lave and Wenger, 1991) (p:98)

Wenger argues that by shadowing fully fledged trades people, apprentices are taking part in 'legitimate peripheral participation' and that it is through this participation that apprentices learn to emulate their mentors' skills, knowledge and behaviour. Only when an apprentice has succeeded in emulating the tradesperson fully can the apprentice be considered for formal entry into their trade. By becoming a skilled worker, the apprentice is moving from legitimate peripheral participation into full membership of the community of practice of their trade and only then will they be recognised by others in that community as 'belonging'. Their 'belonging' to this community of practice is demonstrated by the extent to which the ex-apprentice behaves according to the 'rules' of their trade community. Accordingly, those apprentices who do not satisfy the criteria for full membership of the skilled community remain 'outsiders' or 'others' and never fully belong. This background is relevant to my research project because of my proposition that higher education leadership operates as communities of practice which women (and men) infiltrate when learning leadership. Traditions, organisational structures, policies and practices, as well as local knowledge all contribute to establishing community practices and my research enquires into how these come together to form the ecosystem of higher education leadership communities of practice of masculinities.

Having said this, communities of practice theory recognises that we are all always learning and therefore 'mutual engagement, joint enterprise and shared repertoire' are never fixed. This is important for the idea of my application of communities of practice to my emancipatory research project exploring higher education gendered leadership cultures because it suggests that things can and do change over time and that members of leadership communities of practice (whatever their membership status) have some capacity for agency and resistance. Interestingly because of their experiences of the education world, my research participants were familiar with the concept of communities of practice although they had not, in the main, seen their learning of leadership in these terms.

2.3.2 Communities of practice of masculinities

Legitimate participation in communities of practice of masculinities in many societies confers, through the patriarchal dividend, significant benefits such as, for example, higher earnings, higher levels of education, greater access to political power in public life and greater personal power in the private realm. Given how the literature has pointed to women as 'the other', my research has been exploring whether higher education 'society' operates in this way too and, therefore, how well might gendered leadership cultures across higher education be interpreted and made sense of in terms of communities of practice of masculinities? This would have implications for women, and men, and how they learn leadership gender performativity in order to 'belong' to this leadership exclusive community or 'club'.

Recently, Paechter applied this concept of communities of practice to the learning of gender (Paechter, 2007, Paechter, 2003b). She argues that we are all apprentices from birth when it comes to making and doing our gender. However, she is not happy with the term 'gender' overall, because she now thinks it has become too fixed, similar to the term sex, so prefers to use 'femininities' and 'masculinities' wherever possible in her work. Paechter agrees with Butler (2006) that femininities and masculinities are performative and argues that just like other apprenticeships they represent a stylised repetition of acts and a social temporality and therefore:

> We do not just get up in the morning and decide that today we will be particular kinds of men and women; we slip into our roles, so imperceptibly that most of the time we do not even notice. It is only when we find ourselves performing, or attempting a masculinity or femininity that for some reason fails to 'fit' a particular social situation (being non-macho in a pub full of rugby players to coin a stereotype) that this performative aspect is brought home to us as we subtly, or not so subtly, change our behaviour to fit in better with the situation in which we find ourselves.
>
> (Paechter, 2003b) (p:69)

Like apprenticeships, femininities and masculinities can be interpreted as shared histories of learning involving continuity and discontinuity – a job never done or unfinished business – so that communities of practice signify the continuous nature of learning. We are always learning about our belonging to communities of practice of femininities and masculinities and throughout our lives will 'belong' to a number of communities of femininities and masculinities practice simultaneously in different life contexts and:

> This should help us to understand not only how different masculinities and femininities are performed in different social situations, but, in relation to this, how communities of practice of masculine and feminine practices are established, perpetuated and changed.
>
> (Paechter, 2003b) (p:71)

Perhaps 'belonging' is such a strong human need that 'apprentice' higher education leaders necessarily learn to perform in accordance with the prevailing leadership culture in order for them to be identified and correspondingly treated by this community as a legitimate member. So diversity of behaviour will be discouraged because of this need to be recognised (by themselves and others) as a member of the club whereby:

> Membership of such localised communities of masculine and feminine practices are important components of individual and group identity. Knowing that one belongs to a particular community of practice is an important aspect of understanding one's identity.
>
> (Paechter, 2003b) (p:73)

> Consequently, learning how to be a full participant is about learning how to be, and communities of masculinity and femininity practice are no exception to this. Learning full participation in a community of masculinity or femininity practice is about learning one's identity and how to enact it.
>
> (Paechter, 2006) (p:17)

Similarly, people learn to be leaders within higher education through leadership communities of practice and these communities predominantly perform masculinities. Consequently, these leadership communities of practice of masculinities define their membership by initiating emerging leaders as novices, apprentices and (for some) full members. According to Paechter, the model of initiation into group practices works well for the learning of femininities and masculinities because it:

> Treats identities as relational and as a nexus of multi-membership. This makes identity dynamic; we are not just men and women but are also members of ethic, classed, family and work communities with which we work in constructing our varying and variable identities,

reflecting the Foucaultian idea that the self is the site of multiple practices.

(Paechter, 2006) (p:14)

By using communities of practice of masculinities to interpret the learning of leadership we can allow for the fluidity of boundaries across and between different femininities and masculinities and for local and negotiated ways of being. We can also recognise how resistant these communities are to change because of their continuous nature, which means where resistance does occur, new communities are formed but the old ones remain intact. Similarly, we can understand how and why leaders perform the gender they do, not as something they arbitrarily take up and enact but as specific to context because they are constrained partly by leadership communities of practice (of masculinities) of which they are a part.

2.3.3 Higher education leadership as communities of practice of masculinities

Morley writes extensively about the silences around what I am proposing as leadership as communities of practice of masculinities in higher education (Morley, 2005). There is evidence from my participants that these silences are embedded and go unchallenged, which endorses my own experience of leadership development within several universities. Bagilhole and White found that their respondents dislike the 'macho, boys club' style of management teams. However, they reflected, why is it that the people who dislike this behaviour do not challenge it? Although they recognise that women who are assertive and challenging in this way risk being labelled as 'trouble makers', what they could not understand is why it is that men who find these leadership styles unacceptable do not challenge them either (Bagilhole and White, 2011). My theoretical framework around higher education leadership communities of practice of masculinities would help explain this conundrum. These communities do not include men *per se*, nor are all women excluded. Instead, higher education leadership communities of practice of masculinities prevail because they endorse and reward certain types of masculinities, mostly the hegemonic type. Both women and men, who do not fit in with this 'source of coherence' of the senior leadership community in which women (and men) have to embrace mutual engagement, joint enterprise and a shared repertoire of performances, will be excluded and at best remain in 'legitimate peripheral participation'.

One reason higher education leaders may not resist these leadership communities of practice of masculinities is because individuals gain power from participation in them, and even though resistance is possible, the benefits of conformity often outweigh the alternative. Challenging gender binaries and disrupting hegemonic masculinities at work is critical to diversity (Knights and Kerfoot, 2004). This is highlighted in the data analysis chapters when participants discuss unimpressive masculinities leadership and 'fitting in'. Thus, leadership communities of practice of masculinities perpetuate because 'full participants are able to act as definers of reality and thus identity' (p:16); they are constantly regulated mutually, panoptically, symmetrically and asymmetrically and because power relations and knowledge forms are integral to them (Paechter, 2006). Paechter argues that there are certain features pertaining to communities of practice of masculinities and I have analysed these in relation to my study in order to justify proposing her thinking as the foundation for my theoretical framework around *higher education leadership communities of practice of masculinities.*

To begin with, Paechter argues that femininities and masculinities are performative, socially constructed and temporal which means that there is a multiplicity of femininities and masculinities inhabited and enacted by different people and by the same people at different times (Paechter, 2003b). This is apparent from the findings of the present study where my participants talk about the behaviour and characteristics of themselves and their colleagues within a fluid spectrum spanning femininities and masculinities (which although they did not initially use, the terms 'femininities and masculinities' were comfortable with them once I had introduced this language).

Paechter (ibid) uses the idea of communities of practice (sites of learning) as a way of thinking about the formation and perpetuation of localised femininities and masculinities, and argues that femininities and masculinities can be treated as communities of practice. Thus, leadership in higher education constitutes communities of practice because people are learning how to do leadership through these leadership communities of practice. Moreover, leadership operates as communities of practice of masculinities in the main, because learning leadership in higher education means learning masculinities leadership. Just as children and young people learn what it is to be feminine or masculine through legitimate peripheral participation, according to Paechter, so people working in higher education learn how to be leaders and do leadership through a similar process, although with the key expectation that learning leadership means learning masculinities.

Paechter (2006) argues that power and knowledge are bound up with femininity and masculinity to such an extent that different power/knowledge forms are seen as feminine and masculine and are used differentially in gendered power relations; to sustain these gendered power relations requires 'girls' and 'boys' to behave differently from birth, something for which they are rewarded. The literature and my findings endorse the proposition about gendered leadership cultures within higher education and that this culture perpetuates gendered power relations where we require women and men to behave differently and for which they are rewarded accordingly.

Knowing that you belong to particular communities of practice is an important aspect of understanding your identity. Wenger (1998) analyses identity under five dimensions which Paechter relates to the doing of femininities and masculinities. First, identity as the negotiated experience of self suggests multi membership of femininities and masculinities communities of practice and thus multiple forms of identity and the multiple positioning of individuals within power/knowledge relations. Second, identity as community membership through mutual engagement, joint enterprise and shared repertoire where it is shared repertoire that is most important for femininities and masculinities. Third, identity is seen as a learning trajectory where identity (feminine or masculine) is a work in progress, constantly renegotiated and fundamentally temporal. Fourth, identity as a nexus of multi membership has the advantage of taking into account the ways in which individuals inhabit overlapping femininities and masculinities which change according to time, location and social context and allow us to consider how we manage and understand the interrelationships between these. Lastly, identity is an intersection between the local and the global whereby femininities and masculinities however local in focus are influenced by the media, popular culture and wider society.

Similarly I argue, along with Paechter (2006), that reification – the process of taking practices and using them as community markers of one kind or another, for example by marking full participation with badges and membership cards or formalising practices into procedures – works for communities of practice of femininities and masculinities generally as well as in the leadership workplace too with such things as 'uniforms' and status symbols like car parking spaces and private offices.

Paechter (2003b) applies Wenger's criteria for communities of practice to her theory around communities of practice of masculinities, which can be extrapolated so as to underpin my theoretical framework about higher education leadership communities of practice of masculinities.

To begin with, the negotiation of meaning whereby communities of practice of femininities and masculinities are involved in the constant production, reproduction and negotiation of what it is to be a woman or a man. Someone who does not share with the full members of a community of feminine or masculine practice what it means to be female or male in that context will only ever be practising legitimate peripheral participation. This suggests that there is a negotiation of meaning in higher education leadership communities of practice because women and men are learning what it is to be leaders and that being successful leaders invariably requires performing masculinities.

With regard to the criteria around practice as a source of coherence, Paechter (ibid) argues that this results in a shared repertoire of practices which are acceptable to communities of practice of femininities and masculinities (she gives the example of boys not crying but expressing anger publicly). This suggests that there are shared repertoires of leadership practices which are acceptable to higher education leadership communities of practice and that these more often than not involve masculinities practices (my participants give examples of men talking more/louder than many women in most forums and women not feeling comfortable crying in meetings).

Paechter (ibid) interprets 'Communities of practice as a learning process' insofar as communities represent dynamic shared histories of learning where at no point is practice fully learned and where most people are being members of several communities simultaneously. Thus, femininities and masculinities are in a state of perpetual learning. Higher education leadership communities of practice are in continual flux, changing and being made and done throughout time. Equally, members of higher education leadership communities of practice are also members of several other communities of practice at the same time in both their public and private spaces and, therefore, leadership is in a state of perpetual learning. I suggest that leadership performed through masculinities is a learning and changing process too and consequently argue that this supports my endeavours for a critical mass of femininities (and feminism) in leadership communities.

For the penultimate criterion, practice as a boundary, Paechter (ibid) suggests that femininities and masculinities are defined in part by the 'othering' of outsiders and whilst femaleness and maleness are clearly marked on our bodies, which makes it more likely that communities of practice of which we become members will be correspondingly feminine or masculine, this relation is neither direct nor straightforward. Whereas with my theoretical framework of higher education leadership communities of practice of masculinities, whilst I suggest that they operate as a boundary, this demarcation is not necessarily created by whether you have female or male bodies but rather, as to whether you are learning and performing leadership masculinities. Clearly, the boundary works in leadership communities of practice by 'othering' leadership femininities which, once again, surfaced through the analysis of my data in Chapter 5.

Finally, practice as local, which Paechter (ibid) interprets as meaning that power/knowledge relations within and between localised feminine and masculine communities of practice contribute to and underpin power/knowledge relations within and between wider practices, thus creating a symbiotic relationship between the local nature of communities of practice and their relationship to wider communities and social structures. Higher education leadership communities of practice are by their very nature local in form, culminating at the micro level across institutions. However, they are also steeped in the context for leadership across higher education (such as Universities UK [UUK], HEFCE, Russell Group) and the wider context of leadership in society. This is why I have been keen to situate my research within this wider context of leadership, masculinities and power across all sectors in the UK, not just education.

In summary, members of higher education leadership communities of practice of masculinities have to work hard all the time on earning their membership and 'belonging', as all memberships are temporal. Consequently, masculinities have to be repeatedly demonstrated to maintain the status quo and to keep the club 'in tact'. Invariably, because masculinities are about gender relations they are conferred by men and confirmed by women. This usually means that the boundaries of communities of practice of masculinities are policed from the inside whereby the existing members of the community act as gatekeepers to the introduction of new members, or graduating apprentices. It has been invaluable to hear the voices of women vice chancellors on whether, and if so how, they interpret their lived experiences of leadership as gendered and gendering higher education leadership communities of practice.

2.4   Achieving a critical mass of women at the top: *'Fixing the women'*

Social sciences have adopted the term (and definition of) 'critical mass' during conversations around social change (Collins, 2013). Familiar discourse includes 'there needs to be a critical mass of people before change will happen' or 'once you get a critical mass it makes a difference'. It appears that it is not necessary to quantify a critical mass of people, as there is an assumption that it will be obvious when this is reached. More importantly for this study around the learning of higher education leadership:

> To make a difference in the way leadership is modelled researched and practiced women must attain a critical mass in all the different contexts in which they exercise leadership...three or more women on boards make a difference whereas one or two do not.
>
> (Klenke, 2011)

Achieving a critical mass of women in senior leadership roles is fundamental to changing the representation of women in leadership overall (Bickley, 2010, Butler, 2013, Kramer et al., 2006, Vinnicombe et al., 2008). Critical mass is defined as at least 30 per cent, or a minimum of three women directors on a board of ten members. At this rate women cease to be tokens, or 'the other', as people stop seeing them as women and instead start evaluating their work as managers (Kanter, 1977). Until this critical mass of an underrepresented group is reached often their members are labelled as 'token' representatives and their inclusion in the mainstream (malestream) seen as tokenism. So when does tokenism become a critical mass? Kanter suggests that when the non-dominant members of a particular group reach 35 per cent, which she refers to as 'the tilted group', they become more than 'tokens' and constitute a 'minority', in which they are able to affect the culture of the group. Her terminology of 'a minority' appears contradictory to a critical mass but she argues that a genuine minority group, for example in UK politics the Liberal Democrats (within the coalition), can really influence culture and decision making (Kanter, 1977). It is interesting that Kanter suggests 35 per cent as the minimum membership of a 'tilted group' because during my data generation, several participants defined their idea of a critical mass of women at the top as being 30 to 35 per cent and that this would make a difference to the gendered cultures.

Whilst ever women remain as tokens within an organisation, sector or society, Kanter's tokenism theory makes certain predictions about the inevitability of the outcomes for women. With regard to women in the workplace, Kanter's theory predicts that women executives encounter at least six negative consequences that can be barriers to their career success and advancement. These are: that women may feel that they are not a good fit with the male dominated culture at senior management levels or that they need to change in some way to fit in; that in work groups with skewed gender ratios the dominant group (men) tend to heighten cultural boundaries by exaggerating their camaraderie, emphasising their differences from the token women and excluding women from informal interactions where critical information is exchanged; that they receive less mentoring and support (or less effective mentoring) than male executives (bearing in mind that relationships with white male mentors are associated with career success anyway); that women are more dependent on formal organisational career management processes and depend more upon formal meritocratic procedures such as consideration of objective qualifications whereas men make greater use of informal networks to secure promotion offers; that women are more likely to be viewed stereotypically, jobs tended to be segregated by gender, there is a tendency to bias staffing decisions and career tracking in favour of the dominant group (men) and that both male and female managers may select men over comparably qualified women for upper level managerial positions; and that women may have difficulty obtaining opportunities for geographic mobility such as overseas assignments because of stereotypic assumptions that they are unwilling to relocate because of dual career family considerations (Kanter, 1977).

There is a clear association between the perpetuation of leadership communities of practice of masculinities and the absence of a critical mass, a tilted group, of women at the top. So, Kanter's six negative consequences endorse my interpretation of the implications and experiences for many women of leadership communities of practice of masculinities which I have explored in detail elsewhere and which I also debate through the data analysis in Chapter 6. Also, as I have positioned my research within the wider conversation around 'the missing women' the impact of Kanter's tokenism and correspondingly leadership communities of practice of masculinities spreads across sectors beyond education. However, it is important to stress here that I am not suggesting a critical mass of women necessarily means a critical mass of feminist women. Nor am I essentialising all women. Nevertheless, more women in visible leadership roles has the potential to expand the diversity within these leadership communities of practice of masculinities which in turn makes a difference to the leadership cultures overall, as other commentators agree (Butler, 2013, Erkut et al., 2008, Kramer et al., 2006).

There is not much difference noted in dynamics when women constitute fewer than 25 per cent of a community, at 30–35 per cent there becomes a 'feeling of normality' and once representation is greater than

35 per cent a difference in decision making is noticed (McGregor, 2011). Lone women on boards are not listened to or taken seriously and may be expected to represent all women's views (Erkut et al., 2008). Even two women, although demonstrating that all women are not the same, can still be treated as 'tokens' and a critical mass of three or more are needed for the board to be 'normalised' (Erkut et al., 2008).

The benefits of a critical mass in politics are twofold: the effect on the way politics is done and the policy issues that are prioritised; and greater engagement with civil society organisations (Osmond, 2009). Higher education might learn from this ethical finding given its social justice agenda. The ethical conversation has been revisited since the economic downturn brought about by the financial crash. (Desvaux et al., 2010, Ferrary, 2009). The lack of women in fund management could contribute to further uncertainty and instability in the markets whereas achieving a critical mass of women would enhance sustainability in this precarious yet vital industry (Kramer et al., 2006, Zehner and Basch, 2009). Kramer et al. showed that a critical mass of three or more women can cause a fundamental change in the boardroom and enhance corporate governance. Women engage in less discussion and debate on high risk strategic board decisions (and thus vote with the majority on such matters) in the absence of them forming a critical mass (Butler, 2013). Organisations with women on their board consistently outperform those which only have male directors suggesting that greater effort across the board, a better mix of leadership skills, access to a wider pool of talent and better reflection on the consumer are the main reasons why greater gender diversity makes a difference (Phillips, 2012). The dual justifications for promoting a critical mass of women in business are about challenging masculine bias in beliefs about leadership and addressing group dynamics that operate in small groups (Vinnicombe et al., 2008). Loss of women results in a wastage of talent and inefficiency whereas increasing the participation rate of women in senior roles and engaging women in positions of influence brings competitive advantage. Focus on short term business drivers and masculine cultures help to exclude women from executive roles and this has the potential to impact on organisational performance (Bickley, 2010). Ultimately, sex and gender roles are more stereotypical and more problematic in organisations with relatively low proportions of senior women (Ely, 1995) and it is not just the number of women in organisations that determine the gendered culture or otherwise. Instead it is the number of women in powerful and influential roles or as Ely calls them 'sex integrated firms' that really makes a change to the gendered nature of organisational cultures.

Thus, I have explored gendered leadership cultures in higher education within a theoretical framework of leadership communities of practice of masculinities and, in particular, how women thrive in these cultures especially what may make a difference to the representation of women in senior leadership thereby achieving a 'critical mass'. Critical mass is significant for long term, sustainable change in the representation of women at the top, as are 'critical acts' (Chesterman and Ross-Smith, 2006). Without critical mass and critical acts, there will only be piecemeal and incremental change, playing around at the edges and never tackling the real issue. These critical acts refer to symbolic positive action interventions such as those encouraged by the Athena SWAN agenda (Forum, 2010) which importantly does not confuse positive action with positive discrimination (O'Cinneide, 2012). The absence of such positive action as 'crucial drivers for change' will have a negative impact on gender equality in universities (Morley, 2014).

My motivation within my feminism frame is clear – there are structural inequalities in higher education, and elsewhere, that need to be addressed before step change can happen. For women to be better represented at the top, leadership communities of practice of masculinities have to be challenged and clearly a way to do this is to broaden the diversity of leadership communities overall. Achieving a critical mass of women in senior leadership will contribute significantly to widening diversity (notwithstanding my reluctance to essentialise women or equate more women with more feminist women) and, given the research about the number of years this will take to happen incrementally, I maintain that one way to quicken that pace is a campaign which addresses structural inequalities. I accept this doesn't fit well with poststructural feminism although I am happy to take a 'pick and mix' approach to feminist epistemology in order to serve my emancipatory agenda (Francis, 1999, Francis, 2002). I have sympathy therefore with Connell and her seminal work on gender and power where she argues that poststructural feminism does not need to reject structuralist notions of power. Rather, those structures are temporal themselves and cause and are caused by relationships and so as such are subject to change by practice. What matters here though, is the extent to which structures can be changed in favour of the disadvantaged as:

Majorities matter if the process of social change is to come under conscious human control... structures cannot be levered into new shapes without mutations of grassroots practice. But majorities do not fall from heaven. They have to be constructed ... the lion in the path is the calculus of interests. In a gender order where men are advantaged and women are disadvantaged, major structural reform is, on the face of it, against men's interests ... whether the gender order's tendencies towards crisis have gone far enough to provide a basis for majorities committed to major structural reform is perhaps the key strategic question radical politics now faces.

(Connell, 1987) (pp:285–286)

What I take from Connell with regard to the importance of the critical mass for penetrating leadership communities of practice of masculinities is what she calls 'majorities matter'. Thus majorities (critical mass, tilted group), by virtue of their practice can and do lever major structural and cultural reform. Most importantly though, these majorities have to be constructed because they will not happen otherwise and 'they do not fall from heaven' or arise as a gift. It is against the interests of the dominant group, the leadership communities of practice of masculinities, to reform the gender order structures. This endorses my argument that without a critical mass of women (and diversity more generally) there will be no real change to higher education gendered leadership cultures and that even having recognised this, action will be needed to make this come about. It will not happen without because the vested interests of the dominant group (invariably 'default man' (Perry, 2014)) playing out through leadership communities of practice of masculinities will resist, either directly or indirectly, and because of the myth of the gender neutral culture (Osmond, 2009).

Norway has been driving the agenda for change in the representation of women in leadership communities of practice for some time now and the Norwegian approach is underpinned throughout by compulsory targets in all sectors, including the research sector which incorporates higher education. The quota position enacted by Norway public policy (and other countries following suit) is reminiscent of Connell's on majorities discussed above. The interests of the establishment are not going to willingly welcome change. Instead 'majorities' or 'tilted groups' have to be legislated for and this legislation has to be underwritten and funded accordingly. Within the Norwegian higher education and research sector several million Kroner have been allocated to their BALANSE programme (Balance in senior positions and research management with the objective to improve the gender balance in senior academic positions) (Rustad and Ryste, 2010). And there is an annual prize of two million kroner to the institution making the most difference. Enhancing the quality of higher education and research is the key justification for pursuing gender equality (Rice, 2014). Rice argues that there can only be three possible reasons why his university was suffering from a lack of senior women – they are not good enough, they don't want it or something discriminatory is happening in the institution – and he is convinced it can only be the latter (Rice, 2014). Similarly, Norwegian politician Ansgar Gabrielsen justifies their quota regime when he says:

> What's the point in pouring a fortune into educating girls, and then watching them exceed boys at almost every level if, when it comes to appointing business leaders in top companies these are drawn from just half the population – friends who have been recruited on fishing and hunting trips or from within a small circle of acquaintances? It's all about tapping into valuable under-utilised resources.
>
> (Gilmour, 2010)

So are conditions conducive for women (at home and at work) to them getting on and moving up the leadership ladder in order to satisfy this critical mass? My study does not dwell directly on the private space of women and its impact, or otherwise, on their careers. This is not to say the research ignores the private space; in fact many women in my study willingly discussed their family circumstances and I share some of this data and discuss this in the analysis chapters. However, I am mainly concerned with the private space in respect of how it plays out for leadership communities of practice of masculinities. Also, my participants have all been of a certain generation and it is hard to see whether and how much their experiences are relevant to younger emerging women academic leaders. Notwithstanding this, some recent research that has studied people who graduated with a PhD in the USA late in the 1990s and who moved into academic careers clarifies the position that:

> Marriage does play a role in the gendering of academic career outcomes. Men with PhDs who are married (or partnered) to mates without professional-level degrees gain tenure more quickly than all others. These men are not only gaining tenure faster than other men, but they are gaining tenure at the most prestigious universities at higher rates than women. Women whose partners are less educated do not realize the same career gains from this configuration as men.... advancement to the highest levels in the faculty hierarchy is still, in part, dependent on a particular marital configuration that is not available to women.
>
> (Morrison et al., 2011) (p:550)

Also, with regard to the impact of motherhood on career advancement:

> It is noteworthy that McElrath's (1992) women faculty respondents indicated that career interruptions were due to their spouse's employment three times as often as due to maternity... studies showing positive associations for women between marriage and academic careers and motherhood and academic careers have been integrated into the literature as evidence for an expansionist view of work and family roles.
>
> (Morrison et al., 2011) (p:530)

This expansionist theory focuses on the psychologically positive aspects of functioning within multiple roles, so rather than being a disadvantage for academics with multiple identities there can be a positive energising effect, although this is not endorsed by the ongoing conversations about the role of women in public and private spaces, even in the 21st century. My participants have successfully negotiated this multiple role tension, although to what extent they believe they have 'missed out' in any of them I cannot say. However, Walkerdine describes the conflict for women between the discourse of the professional individualistic advancement and career dedication with a less conscious discourse of women's desire to be home with children when she argues:

> The feminist discourses and economic necessities through which women workers have been constituted clash badly with other, older discourses that have powerfully formed feminine subjectivities. The expectation and desire for independence can conflict with a deep-rooted desire to take time out to have children, to stay home to rear them and to be 'looked after'.
>
> (Walkerdine et al., 2001) (p:81)

Similarly, Smulyan conducted a longitudinal study of women students training to be teachers and doctors and learned from them about the tensions and conflict between social and cultural definitions and discourses of success, work and self (Smulyan, 2004). I accept that private space cannot be separated from the public one and, of course, this is pertinent to women getting on in their careers. So for example, the gendered career structure and the organisational culture of the health sector and medical profession create a role conflict between personal and professional lives which in turn create barriers to the career progression of women (Miller and Clark, 2008). I contest that this is not dissimilar in higher education either, where women belong to a number of communities of practice concurrently and these may be in conflict with each other. One of my vice chancellor participants even aligned herself with the 'what women academics need is a wife' quote. It is probably not a coincidence to find that many women academics in senior leadership roles in higher education have no children (Breakwell and Tytherleigh, 2008), or no partner, or a partner who is 'retired' or older stepchildren, and that this demographic occurs for women at the top across other sectors too.

Hewlett, writing in the *Harvard Business Review*, focuses on returning women who go 'off the ramps' in some part of their career for whatever reason and need to get back 'on the ramps' when this stage in their private space has passed. She found that many professional women find it difficult getting 'back on the ramps' and places the onus on employers to stop the brain drain from highly qualified, committed women who need to time out of the workplace (Hewlett and Luce, 2005). This is interesting for my study because none of my participants have worked less than full time (except for maternity leave) even though within that commitment they have worked flexibly. According to one of my participants, it is high time that higher education was more accepting of haphazard employment track records. Several of my participants commented that women need to be smarter about working flexibly discreetly; in other words they see many of their women colleagues being too open and honest about their other commitments when instead, as long as they are doing the work and meeting all expectations, the flexible cultures of higher education are such that someone can incorporate caring responsibilities into full-time employment. Although for many women in the workplace, getting on in leadership communities of practice of masculinities can mean merely doing what it takes to get the job done. Bilimoria talks about a phase of 'pragmatic endurance' between the ages of 36 and 45 and thinks that women in this phase are:

> Operating in production mode, doing what it takes to get it done.... the staggering impact of negative organisations and managers, and discrimination and sexual harassment combine to produce a bleak environment for many mid-career women.
>
> (Bilimoria and Piderit, 2007) (p:183)

So much so that women are underrepresented in senior leadership because there are three 'subtle problems' faced by women academics: firstly, their relative powerlessness as minorities within academia; secondly, male domination of knowledge; and thirdly, the conflicting demands of greedy institutions – work and family (Acker and Armenti, 2004). Acker has been writing about the position of women in higher education for some time now, finding that structures, policies and practices across the university system work to the detriment of women and that no organisational support network exists (Acker, 1992). Even 30 years ago she was asking the question 'is higher education fair to women' (Acker and Piper, 1984). More recently she has found that many women academics are working harder and sleeping less (Acker and Armenti, 2004) because of their attempt to overcome issues and anxieties they have around children, career and evaluation as well as their general fatigue and stress. I admire Acker's work because she situates 'the woman's problem' within the wider context of 'their powerlessness as minorities' and 'the male domination of knowledge' both of which I maintain may be addressed to some extent by diluting leadership communities of practice of masculinities. I see Acker's position as another way to express the 'fixing the women, fixing the organisation, and fixing the knowledge' trilogy (Schiebinger, 1999, Morley, 2013b) which is important because it acknowledges the structural inequalities contributing to women's underrepresentation in leadership. Influenced by Schiebinger and Morley, I suggest that there are three approaches needed to address the underrepresentation of women in higher education leadership. Paying attention to women themselves (fixing the women), paying attention to the structural issues within institutions (fixing the organisation) and paying attention to gendered ways of knowing (fixing the knowledge). Nevertheless, much of the literature explores 'the woman's problem' so I do consider this later in the chapter.

Accordingly, Airini recently studied 26 women in New Zealand to find out what helped and hindered their advancement in university roles and of the five key themes that emerged only one was to do with the private space, despite the attention sometimes given in the literature to the private space (Airini et al., 2011). The themes were: work relationships; university environment; invisible rules; proactivity and personal circumstances. The study attempts to identify structural factors in universities rather than deficits in women themselves that help and hinder their advancement and also aims to underpin the development of programmes supporting women's advancement in leadership roles. From my perspective it reflects the most recent movement for researchers aiming to divert the attention from 'fixing the women' to focusing instead on the structures, policies and practices that deny women their leadership voice, thus 'fixing the organisation' and 'fixing the knowledge'.

In this vein, there are feminist perspectives on restructuring policy in higher education and this in turn links to my gender mainstreaming lens discussed above (Allan et al., 2010). Although, there is some data coming through from institutions now which provides encouraging evidence about the success of applications made by women for senior leadership roles. Dandridge, in an online Guardian Higher Education article (2011), comments upon the evidence that women are more likely to succeed in applications for senior posts, the problem is that women don't apply in the same numbers as men. Maybe this is because of what Chesterman (2005) calls 'undoable jobs' and I look more closely at the work of Chesterman and Ross below. Suffice to say, Priola's (2007) research endorses this notion of 'undoable jobs' combined with the private space because only two of her participants had children, and two of those who did not have a family declared they had made a definite choice not to. Also two had moved away from their partners to take the promotion and did not think they could have done such a big job otherwise. The main finding is that women put everything into their work and that they don't think dual career families are workable, especially given the general acknowledgement that it is rare for anyone to become a vice chancellor in the UK without being a professor beforehand (another undoable job?) and so already a leading academic in their own research field anyway. It is this pathway to becoming a vice chancellor that my research explores in terms of challenging the genderisation of emerging leaders, penetrating higher education leadership communities of practice of masculinities and building the gender capacity of the 'talent pool' from which the sector might eventually produce fair representation at the top. Otherwise many women are taking day to day decisions (be they rational or emotional) which in a piecemeal way contribute to predicting their future career opportunities. Women are the 'volunteers' in the sector – a call for staff to volunteer over and above their contract more often than not elicits women academics, not men (Middlehurst, 1993). Volunteering on good causes takes time, time which is then not available to dedicate to more career orientated work. Men, Middlehurst found, on the whole are much more strategic about their career plan and ambitions and do not allow 'noises off' to deter them from their goals. Masculinity has a capacity to think about oneself and put oneself before anything else. For a woman, simply agreeing (an emotional rather than rational decision perhaps) to edit a less prestigious journal than the one their male colleague edits can be a piece in the jigsaw that makes the difference to their career trajectory. Management and leadership in higher education have traditionally been predominantly male territory thus the figure of the ideal manager is grounded in masculine values (Middlehurst, 1993).

2.4.1   A woman's problem?

Achieving more women at the top, a critical mass of women in senior leadership, can still be seen as a 'woman's problem' rather than one arising from the nature of academia itself or from wider socially created inequalities (Morley, 2005) (particularly in neoliberal times). Women blame themselves for their lack of success in the promotion field, or their inability to cope long term with the conflicting demands of their various priorities. The deficit model goes like this: women are not confident enough; women are not resilient enough; women are not ambitious enough. Fels reflects upon women's complicated relationship with the concept of ambition:

> For these women ambition necessarily implied egotism, selfishness, self-aggrandisement, or the manipulative use of others for one's own ends. Despite the fact that women are more career orientated than at any time in history – and often more clearly ambitious – there is something about the concept that makes them distinctly uncomfortable. These women's denial of their own ambitiousness was particularly striking in contrast to the men I interviewed, who assumed ambition was a necessary and desirable part of their lives. They often chided themselves for lacking sufficient amounts of it. Perhaps even more surprising, the very women who deplored ambition in reference to their own lives freely admitted to admiring it in men. If ambition was, by definition, self-serving and egotistical, why was it not only acceptable but desirable for men.
>
> (Fels, 2004) (p:5)

For Bagilhole and White in their cross-nation and cross-cultural study of higher education the similarities between countries was much more noticeable and remarkable than the differences, with homosociobility and the perception of women 'as the problem' recurring over and over again (Bagilhole and White, 2011). Women and men have been found to describe and value career success differently too. The women managers in Sturges's study:

> Were more likely than the men to describe what success meant to them with reference to internal criteria, especially accomplishment

and achievement, and intangible criteria, in particular personal recognition. For all of the women...success defined in terms of achievement, personal recognition or influence transcended material career success.

(Sturges, 1999) (p:247)

And:

For most of the men, on the other hand, the position in the hierarchy which they attained was used as a measure of their career success, be it for reasons of status or influence. (p:247)

Thus, in the context of gendered leadership, organisational cultures legitimise women's positions at the lower levels of the hierarchy and portrays managerial jobs as primarily masculine (Deem, 2003). For some time now there has been recognition that people's perception about the requirements for being an effective leader and manager and the match of these requirements with masculine characteristics is very strong; thus, it must be 'a woman's problem' and we need to 'fix the women'. This has been coined 'think manager, think male' (Schein and Davidson, 1993, Schein et al., 2006). Schein studied people's perceptions around management by asking women and men to rate behaviours of managers and leaders on a femininities and masculinities spectrum. Interestingly, not only do a majority of men consider those defined as masculinities behaviours to be the best fit for management and leadership but so also do the majority of the women. Coleman also talks about essentialist stereotypical leadership styles although she finds that both women and men declare they adopt feminine leadership behaviours. Perhaps this shows a lack of consciousness 'and may also reflect the current general distrust [within education] of being labelled a feminist' (Coleman, 2006) (p:6). The men and women Coleman found saying they adopt feminine leadership styles were all head teachers and the adjectives they chose were not 'labelled' feminine or masculine but were those associated with the different styles (such as nurturing and competitive). None of my participants talked about feminism until I mentioned it and even then only a couple were happy to adopt this terminology and I discuss this further in the data analysis chapters. Summing up her take on 'the woman's problem' Chesterman concludes:

That women's unwillingness to apply for senior positions remains a difficult issue for universities. It has always been assumed that through equity measures selection and promotion policies have been amended so that they are no longer discriminatory to women, as had been experienced directly by some of our interviewees. Yet clearly more needs to be done. We have identified such issues as lack of confidence, reticence, ambivalence, seeking balance, and resistance as playing a part in women's avoidance of senior jobs.

(Chesterman et al., 2005) (p:178)

And Morley considers that:

Women are often discursively framed as problem areas. With the exception of gender sensitisation programmes, men and masculinities are rarely problematised or perceived in need of development and training. There are silences about the forms that masculinity takes for initiatives to change higher education and the way in which resistance can constantly mutate. There are many essentialised observations about women's qualities and preferred styles of working. Sometimes a social constructionist approach is taken, particularly in relation to women's career development. Career progress, ambition and self-interest are sometimes seen as unfeminine as they imply desire, greed and attention to the self.

(Morley, 2005) (p:116)

In summary, this effort of 'fitting in' positions ambitious women in a double bind whereby masculine models of leadership are out of reach (Catalyst, 2007, Francis, 2010, Fitzgerald, 2013). Satisfying the greedy institutions of work and attending to domestic and family concerns places a significant burden on women academics, although conversely women without children are often penalised too by expectations they will cover for other women with (Acker and Armenti, 2004, Bascom-Slack, 2011, Cummins, 2005, Hewlett, 2005). Performing femininities excludes women from 'the boys club' yet performing as 'one of the boys' is frowned upon also (Acker, 2010, Eveline, 2005). So invariably leadership roles become 'undoable' jobs for women (Chesterman et al., 2005), although inevitably discourses emerge about 'fixing the women' instead, as though women are homogeneous (Bilge, 2010). There has been a pervading sense that if only women became more resilient, more confident, more ambitious and 'more like a man' the problem would be solved (Schein et al., 2006). More recently, far from blaming women themselves for 'missing' from these undoable jobs it is recognised that their underrepresentation comes from a combination of gendered leadership cultures and women's resistance to these (Clarke and Knights,

2014, Morley, 2013a, Dean et al., 2009, Fotaki, 2013). Consequently Morley asks whether women around the world are dismissing, desiring or being disqualified from higher education leadership (Morley, 2014).

2.4.2 Women helping other women

Within this framing of the issue as a woman's problem should we assume homogeneously that women will help each other out willingly, taking on the role of gender politician, all the time being fully aware of the overriding benefit that achieving more women at the top might have for all women in leadership and throughout the organisation? Because it is common for women to stand in for other women in the academy, when they are away on maternity leave or when their children are ill or when they are away seeing to their family care responsibilities. Ironically, this does not bring about universal 'sisterhood' or enhanced leadership communities of femininities (Mavin and Williams, 2012). Instead, and for single childless women especially:

> Given that they are usually younger and perceived to have more time in lieu of being partnered and in absence of children, they are thought to have more time to spend doing emotion work, serving the mental hygiene function, or caring for colleagues, students, co-workers and parents.
>
> (Cummins, 2005) (p:226)

So instead of women coming together, embracing and reinforcing communities of practice of femininities to support and endorse one another, in a similar fashion to many men within higher education leadership communities of practice of masculinities, women are being positioned as in conflict with other women (Fitzgerald, 2013). Women who have children are in a preferable position to women without (regardless of why these women are childless) and women who are prepared to live the 'masculinities leadership' lifestyle are being positioned as in conflict with women who choose a healthier work-life balance. And that:

> Another aspect of this finds women academics associated with committees that deal with 'students concerns, social issues or routine matters, whereas men are likely to be on committees that deal with policy making or implementation, faculty status or grievances'.
>
> (Cummins, 2005) (p:226)

Thus, because equality policies often focus on the needs of parents, Cummins talks about the 'mommy track' now being preferable to being childless as policies are now working towards making allowances for parenting women. Inevitably this will foster the conflict between groups of women and sow more seeds of resentment and competition rather than sisterhood. This is another of those poststructural, structural arguments. It is not that women are being essentialised or treated as a homogeneous group. The needs of all women in the workplace are different, regardless of whether they are parents or not. What higher education leadership communities of practice of masculinities engender though is conflict and competition between the less powerful and underrepresented groups. This is ironic according to Cummins because for women, whether they are childless or otherwise:

> While on or off the mommy track, the dimensions of human life call women academics in various directions to see to the needs of others. They continue the kin keeping phenomena as do other women.
>
> (Cummins, 2005) (p:227)

Many women in academia, especially openly feminist women, are disappointed by the support they receive from other women. They often come to leadership expecting women to be giving each other a helping hand and to be recognising the barriers that their women colleagues have overcome to make it. Instead they are shocked when this is not the case. Also, women look to women leaders to behave differently than their male counterparts and of course are disappointed when that doesn't happen either. Chesler is one of those with higher education leadership experience herself and she reflects poignantly:

> Forget about academic women helping each other. Some do, but mainly its cutthroat. The mediocre female talents hate and resent the more stellar female talents. They gang up on them and do them in. I no longer say I'm a feminist. For the last twenty years I have seen accomplished and generous women destroyed by other women. The more talented women may not be a loyal member of whatever 'politically correct' clique controls the department...feminist academics have no true standards, only personal interests. Just like the boys.
>
> (Chesler, 2001) (p:381)

And the reliance of female executives in the Lyness study (Lyness and Thompson, 2000) on developing relationships also supports the notion that women who excel in male gender typed roles may in fact be disliked (by women and men) and that they have to overcome these perceptions and build relationships. This is a fascinating aspect of my research because I too was interested in whether the women vice chancellors in my study helped one another out, and maybe even constituted leadership communities of practice of femininities. On the whole my evidence suggests that this doesn't happen and I explore this further in Chapter 6.

In this vein, Blair-Loy and Cech (Wynn, 2012) conducted a research study to examine which factors impact women leaders' perceptions of the glass ceiling. They offered women leader's two explanations – structural and meritocratic – for the lack of women at the top. Over 40 per cent of the women in their sample favoured meritocratic explanations with almost a quarter blaming women themselves saying that they must be overly committed to their families, or have no desire, and that there is nothing actually holding them back. Their conclusion is that the skills that enabled these women to succeed are the reason they are not implementing policies that help other women. I think this suggests they may even be contributing to the re-creation of the glass ceilings they themselves have cracked.

At the time I was conducting my research there were no women at vice chancellor and pro vice chancellor level in a quarter of institutions, and less than 2 per cent of institutions had more than two academic women in academic leadership roles at this level. More surprisingly, in a third of institutions which had a woman vice chancellor there were no other academic women on the executive team. This appears contrary to our expectations of enhanced 'sisterhood' because of the shared experiences of discrimination in the ranks of academia. Instead the 'queen bee' and 'iron lady' syndromes abound, meaning that women reaching senior leadership are as likely to 'go it alone' as they are to engender leadership communities of practice of femininities at the top (Mavin, 2007, Mavin, 2008, Mavin and Williams, 2012). This can defy the expectations of their women colleagues who are hoping that the senior women leaders will act as role models for them and will make it their job to encourage other women to be ambitious whilst being so themselves. So, as I reflected upon earlier, the presence of more women in senior positions is not an accurate measure of higher education cultures either as female cannot be equated with feminism, nor are all feminists reflexive about their location in organisational power relations. Instead, a process of masculinisation can occur for successful women. Morley talks about some interesting findings from her studies around the numbers of women academics in senior leadership positions. Her study revealed that women in higher education have high expectations about the advocacy, representation and support they will get from senior women and that these expectations are almost always not satisfied and as a consequence of their disappointment there is considerable hostility, ambivalence and mistrust of senior women. One university lecturer in her study commented:

> Although one of the pro vice chancellors is a woman, she is hardly the sort of woman who helps other women along, so it's not really been much help to anyone. She is not into feminism at all. She's very much part of the male establishment.
>
> (Morley, 1999) (p:77)

Alongside this lack of sisterhood exists the glass ceiling and the glass cliff syndromes (Heffernan, 2004, Ryan and Haslam, 2005) where even women who make it to professor are not head hunted for that next move or when they are it is because the role they are promoted to is destined to fail. Their visibility is then accentuated because the job doesn't work out (Peterson, 2014). More often than not women in leadership are far more visible when things go wrong and are singled out for their failures rather than their successes. Heffernan traces the patterns and themes underlying women's power choices saying that women's choices are limited and that women can't have it all, although it is possible to find success amidst everything and feel good about it. I am pretty sure none of my participants think that they 'have it all' although they may well argue they have found success and feel good about that.

Consequently, Bagilhole argues strongly for women to help other women, to collaborate and supports others to get on, for them to succeed themselves and then to help other women to succeed. In order for women to thrive women must adopt self-promotion and the promotion of other women (Bagilhole, 2007). Chesterman and Ross-Smith report that their interviewees (81 in total – 50 women and 31 men in five Australian universities where women constituted around 30 per cent of the senior executive) identified the factors crucial for the appointment of women: having a critical mass of other women in senior positions; opportunities to network; encouragement and support from organisational leaders; friendly and collegial environments; and strong organisational commitment to values. Their analysis of the sector revealed that both women and men clearly believe that the presence of women in senior roles had changed management cultures. Inherent is the notion not only of critical mass but 'critical acts'. So when women reached a critical mass both women and men believe that the women's influence (on leadership communities of practice of masculinities) encouraged greater collaboration, more consultative decision-making processes and more collegial workplaces (Chesterman and Ross-Smith, 2005). So one of Chesterman's hypotheses, as she calls them, was very markedly 'that with a high proportion of women in senior roles the cultures at management level would be different to those in male dominated organisations' (she looked at other sectors too but included five universities which had a stated commitment to enhancing the number of women in senior management and had succeeded to a point where women constituted around 30 per cent of the top three levels of the executive).

However, whether women take on the role of gender politician willingly is another reason may be why women are not helping other women to achieve a critical mass in leadership. Some women are not impressed by being seen to be failing if they do not make the promotion of other women one of their goals. 'The invisible job' as Martin calls it, is the pressure upon the woman leader to position herself as a trail blazer for other women (Martin, 1994). The expectation of women, and of men also, that the woman leaders can be relied upon to accomplish this invisible job is idealistic and unrealistic. And for some women doing this invisible job can result in a process of 'othering' anyway for them by being the one who complains and draws attention to the issue.

Nevertheless, Priola found that 'the dominance of women managers has influenced women's work in encouraging them to apply for promotions and in feeling more confident about their contribution' (p:35). On the other hand Priola is not convinced of the idea that a critical mass of women somehow changes the culture although she does admit that:

> Women are not passive recipients of masculine practices and that their responses while creating tensions and conflicts (both at organisational and personal level) may be generating some pockets of change (particularly at department level).
>
> (Priola, 2007) (p:36)

In summary, this chapter has reviewed the literature around higher education gendered leadership cultures and leadership communities of practice of masculinities. The conversation throughout this review has situated this literature within the contemporary context of the prevailing discourses around 'the missing women' in leadership across UK business and the wider community because of the significant role higher education plays in society.

3
Research Methodology and Research Participants

3.1 Ontological and epistemological influences

The key influences and considerations underpinning my research design are those around 'interpretative and qualitative enquiry' and 'feminism and feminist research methodology', and I position my research within the context of these ontological and epistemological journeys below. I hope by including how my research has been influenced in this way readers will sympathise with my journey, one which is forever ongoing.

3.1.1 Ontology and paradigms

My research stems from an interpretive ontological position which recognises a socially constructed, complicated and complex world where higher education leadership is continually evolving and changing and where gender is constantly under construction and never fixed, and where multiple and complex material realities such as leadership cultures are negotiated on an ongoing basis. Ontology refers to the claims or assumptions that a particular approach to social enquiry makes about the nature of social reality and that these claims and assumptions include such things as: what the researcher thinks reality looks like and how they view the world; the researcher's answer to the question of 'what kind of being the human being is'; and how the researcher reflects on the nature of phenomena, or entities or social reality and socially constructed learning theory (Fox, 2006).

This approach to the nature of social reality is normally referred to as a 'paradigm' of positions on the social world, one which contains a researcher's ontological, epistemological and methodological premises (Denzin and Lincoln, 2008). My research sits within the 'interpretive and relativist paradigm' (Denscombe, 2009) and I have become more comfortable working within the interpretive paradigm because it aims to understand people's lived experience from the perspective of people themselves and it focuses on subjective meanings that people attach to their experiences. Also interpretivism looks for the meaning of social actions and emphasises the importance of interpretation and observation in understanding the social world. Those working within the interpretive paradigm see that reality is socially constructed and recognise that experiences occur within social, cultural, historical and personal contexts and that people are individually engaged in acts of sense making. Most crucially, interpretivism argues that research is never value free and that the background and values of researchers themselves also influence the creation of research data (Rugg and Petre, 2007).

Added to which, feminism and feminist research methodology influence my work. As I discussed in Chapter 1, my research has a tendency to sit within structural feminism whilst being largely influenced by post-structuralism too whereby gender and sex are political terms that serve to perpetuate the prevailing system and hierarchy. Challengingly Butler (2006) states:

There is no ontology of gender on which we might construct a politics, for gender ontologies always operate within established political contexts as normative injunctions, determining what qualifies as intelligible sex, invoking and consolidating the reproductive constraints on sexuality, setting the prescriptive requirements whereby sexed or gendered bodies come into cultural intelligibility. Ontology is, thus, not a foundation but a normative injunction that operates insidiously by installing itself into political discourse as its necessary ground. (p:203)

And I agree that my work:

Needs to take into account the access to, and discursive positions available to, different groups that are likely to produce different knowledge. This applies as much to the researcher as to those being researched.

(Skeggs, 1994) (p:27)

3.1.2 Epistemology

As the researcher I saw value in constructionism and was influenced accordingly by this epistemology when I designed the fieldwork, given the nature of my particular enquiry, and this has guided and influenced me throughout all stages of my research. Epistemology relates to issues such as 'what the relationship is between the inquirer and the known' and 'what might represent knowledge or evidence of the social reality that is investigated' and 'what is counted as evidence' (Hennink et al., 2011). Recently there has been controversy surrounding feminist's preference for social constructionist analyses of gendered behaviour (Francis, 2012). This is because the binary position of gender is still taken as the base or superstructure of gender production and those arguing that sexed bodies be separated from gender are also criticised for failing to acknowledge that our bodies define how we are interpreted by others in society and this is inevitable and beyond our control.

Consequently, feminist epistemology is itself temporal and fractured and as such is on its own journey. This journey through feminism informs up-to-date feminist thinking about what's missing, and seeks out the voices that are still not heard despite feminist research methodology (Ryan-Flood and Gill, 2010). So I see that I am working with an epistemology that is itself evolving over time and is contextual and temporal so much so that third wave feminism is being developed and critically appraised by a modern fourth wave which is profiled by everyday sexism and similar online and social media publications, notwithstanding reservations about feminism waves explored recently (David, 2014). Francis has been helpful for me and my epistemological journey by surfacing the tensions between realism and relativism facing feminism and feminists (Francis, 1999, Francis, 2002).

Wharton developed three epistemological approaches to the research of gender which have informed my work (Wharton, 2012). Her individualist approach views gender as part of the person, her interactional approach considers gender to emerge through social interaction (similar to how I am using constructivism) and her institutional approach emphasises how gender is built into organisations, social structures and institutional arrangements. This latter approach is becoming increasingly pertinent to my epistemological journey. There is a recent recognition that gender bias is at play in organisations and that this denies the existence of discrimination despite women's experiences being the contrary (Ely et al., 2011). This 'second generation gender bias' can be seen as different to first generation in that it presumes that equality legislation has overcome discrimination and now expects all opportunities to be equal. By so doing it ignores the impact of structural hegemonic masculinities on organisational cultures, a fundamental reason for the missing women in higher education leadership (Rice, 2014).

Feminist epistemology is presumed to be coming from a place where the status quo needs to be challenged and change needs to happen in order to overcome gender power relations and the gender order. Feminist politics, therefore, addresses the 'otherness' of women and seeks to make change happen. There should be a political point to feminist research (Harding, 1987, Haraway, 1988, Houle, 2009) which is why I adopted feminist epistemology on the understanding that ultimately my research will make a difference and that the knowledge (however situated) growing from it will form a valuable contribution to addressing the 'missing women at the top' conundrum. However, I am mindful about not becoming too obsessed with my epistemological framework in accordance with trends in feminist epistemology because:

> What troubles us most about the current 'romance with epistemology' is that it seems more concerned with attempting to convince the predominantly male academy that a privileged status should be accorded to women's ways of knowing than with enabling us to better discover and understand what is happening in women's lives, and how we might change it.
>
> (Kelly et al., 1994) (p:32)

3.1.3 Researching women

It was vital that as a feminist adopting feminist methodology, and a woman researching women, I approached my research into senior women leaders as carefully and reflexively as possible. I was aware that being 'situated' in the research and my lens of gendered and gendering leadership would influence what I looked for when doing my fieldwork. It has been recognised that the researcher becomes an actor in the fieldwork drama (Meyerson and Kolb, 2000) and I appreciated this when working with others on generating the data.

Historically, many authors have been writing about researching women and women's lives (Behar, 1997, Kelly et al., 1994, Harding, 1987, Maynard and Purvis, 1994, Meyerson and Kolb, 2000, Oakley, 2000, Reay, 1996, Reinharz and Davidman, 1992) and I have been influenced by their concerns for the 'subject' because, as they all agree, whenever women are researching women there are usually power and identity dimensions to consider. It can be argued that women researchers have a high impact on the women they are researching especially if these women see the researchers as more educated and more professional, possibly because the history of researching women's lives has been in social and pathological contexts where researchers are investigating 'social problems' like poverty and abuse. Whether detachment as the researcher is the best approach has also been questioned although, on the other hand, trying to become too friendly with the women you are researching brings its own pitfalls of familiarity and of potentially distorting the data. Nevertheless, Oakley believed this disadvantage to be a risk worth taking for the enriched relationship she encountered by sharing something of herself with those women she was researching as:

> The use of research methods based on 'in-depth' interviewing with selected samples of women, a meticulous, iterative attention to the details of what women say, and forms of analysis dedicated to reproducing all of this as faithfully as possible construct an alternative feminist scholarship.
>
> (Oakley, 1998) (p:13)

In my case, I was not enquiring into women as victims of such things as the poverty trap or domestic violence, nor was I viewing women as a homogeneous group in the academy. Instead I was investigating success – is there anything about the lived experiences of successful women academics that may help me understand and address the underrepresentation of women in UK higher education leadership? Given this context of investigating success and thinking about the integrity of my epistemological framework, I was clear that I needed to talk to these successful women directly. This is one of the ways in which I am meeting a gap in the literature, and a way I am contributing to knowledge, because although much work has studied women in the middle ranks of the academy (Acker, 2010, Bagilhole and White, 2011, Goode and Bagilhole, 1998, Hearn, 2001, Leathwood and Francis, 2006, McTavish and Miller, 2009, Priola, 2007, Saunderson, 2002, Wagner et al., 2008, Wise, 1997), my study set out to approach every women vice chancellor to ask for a face-to-face meeting to discuss their careers. Thankfully, there is evidence to show that many women enjoy being interviewed by women researchers. Similar to Oakley's findings that there is a connection between the researcher and the researched when both are women, Brannen suggests that:

> Participants respond favourably to some methods especially where there is overlap between the concerns of researchers and those of participants, and where both parties are in search of similar explanations.
>
> (Brannen, 1993) (p:329)

Contrary to Oakley I am 'researching the powerful' or 'studying up' as it is often called, always mindful of the Foucaultian interpretation of power. There has been some research around women researching 'powerful' women (Puwar, 1997, Walford, 2011, Williams, 1989) which informed my preparation for interviewing my participants. Puwar is a woman researcher who was interviewing women politicians and who observes the seduction of power and its implications for those people who by the nature of their role acquire powerful identities and this, in turn, impacts upon the knowledge making process. There are a number of issues that are different when women are researching women considered to be 'the powerful' from those when women are researching those considered to be more vulnerable women. For example: it is anticipated that powerful women will have an agenda and will already know what they want to say and are prepared to talk about in the meeting; powerful women are familiar with influencing and persuading others and they may try to behave this way in the research process; and the researcher will have less control overall and this may contaminate the generation and collection of the data. Chesterman was well aware of the implications and practicalities of researching 'powerful' women when she says:

> When we sought funding for this project it was agreed that the three of us would do most of the interviews ourselves and not, as is more common, employ research assistants to undertake this task. The reason for this was the fact that we would be interviewing very senior people. The bulk of our participants were women and, like us, were white Anglo Saxon, university educated and middle aged, so status differences, to this extent, were minimal. Yet in what amounted to almost the reverse of situations where the researcher is in a more powerful position and hence potentially more able to exploit the research participant, we were in reality often in a less powerful position than most of our interviewees. For example we were often kept waiting for long periods of time before interviews commenced. Interviews were frequently cancelled and had to be rescheduled three or four times because the participants had other more urgent appointments. We always went to the office of our participants to conduct the interview so we were in their 'territory' rather than our own.
>
> (Chesterman et al., 2005) (p:165)

Although, interestingly, these logistical issues never arose during my fieldwork. I was never kept waiting for my interview and only once did an interviewee have to reschedule. I am mindful that the researcher role brings some power with it to the research relationship, and I have had a long career in leadership development so I am comfortable working with senior leaders and I had had ten years of experience in higher education, which meant I understood the context and was not intimidated by the jargon and protocols. Despite this, I was aware of the influence of a 'power making' participant, such as that of vice chancellor, on the research process.

Researching only women at the top (and not any of the men) can be interpreted as only seeing a partial picture. It is inevitable that some of the men at this level may well have backgrounds and careers that are relevant to my enquiry about gendered leadership cultures, leadership communities of practice of masculinities and thriving in these. However, after much reflection I was determined that my specific project required this emphasis on successful women. Women's stories about their success and their experiences of higher education leadership cultures are the story here and this story should not be waylaid by me feeling any obligation to talk to men too. Whether my findings lead on to another project incorporating some of the men's stories is open for debate. I am recommending in my conclusions for this research to require follow-up work anyway and this may well be an area for future focus. Notwithstanding this, I can see that by only inquiring into women I can be adding to the argument that it is a woman's problem as:

> They locate the problem in women: women have not been socialised to compete successfully in the world of men, and so they must be taught the skills their male counterparts have acquired as a matter of course.
>
> (Ely et al., 2011) (p:5)

And that we need to 'fix the women' which has never been my intention and my book is testament to this because I maintain that gendered leadership cultures should be the concern of everyone in the sector and 'the men' will need to come on board to tackle it wholeheartedly if real change is to happen. The fledgling HeForShe campaign and the Lean In Together circles reflects this movement as does ongoing research (UNWomen, 2014, Ford et al., 2014).

3.2   Interviewing

Qualitative research is not intended to be representative of the general population and qualitative research cannot measure or test effects, relationships or influences, or identify determinants (Hennink et al., 2011). Whereas quantitative research concentrates on statistics, numbers, counting and uses these type of figures to make projections and assumptions about social phenomena, and there is a debate for feminist researchers about adopting 'malestream', quantitative methods (Hughes and Cohen, 2012). I have been influenced by this admittedly, although this prejudice can lead to the gendering of methodology itself as a social construction (Oakley, 1998). In other words, feminist researchers need to be wary of the influence not only of their ontological and epistemological approaches but also of their methodology and to always take the position that a certain approach or a certain method is gendered before long becomes entrenched and constructed as such.

Qualitative research usually involves methods such as case studies, interviewing, ethnography and observation (Cassell and Symon, 2012). It places the researcher alongside the person/people being researched and as such requires an interaction between the two. These binaries of qualitative and quantitative can, however, limit social researchers in their quest for 'an emancipatory social science' (Oakley, 2000). Consequently I have not been precious about labelling my research as qualitative especially as I have been pursuing an emancipatory project, although the interview method was the most appropriate for my research because it emphasises open-ended, non-leading questions, it focuses on personal experience more than general beliefs and opinions, and it seeks to build a rapport between me as the researcher and my participants (King and Horrocks, 2010, Coleman, 2012a). Thus:

> Qualitative interviewing situates the methodology and method deliberately within the qualitative domain where a broad and holistic approach is taken to the study of social phenomena.
>
> (King and Horrocks, 2010) (p:7)

Generally, interviewing as a qualitative research method in social science has been explored and analysed (King and Horrocks, 2010, Spradley, 1979, Green and Thorogood, 2009) enough for me to have been able to combine my own professional and career knowledge and experience of interviewing with the lessons these researchers have offered me about their work and expertise in their own field.

Bourdieu (1993) argues that interviews must be understood within their 'social praxiology', that is the position of the interviews within the prevailing social, political, commercial and economic times, and I attempted to do just that by studying the micro worlds of senior higher education leaders within broader macro social and cultural contexts. I was fully aware of my reflexive impact as researcher on the research process and believe the interviews to be what Bourdieu calls 'the double reality of the social world' where structuralism and constructionism come together.

Puwar's reflections on interviewing women MPs (Puwar, 1997) have been especially helpful given that they too are 'powerful' women and in her case she felt intimidated and occasionally in awe of her participants, although this was not my experience. I was keen at all times to conduct myself in a highly professional manner and I sense that this approach has been valued and respected by the women I have interviewed. Even, interestingly, the one interview that I was and still am dissatisfied with ended with the vice chancellor praising me on my professional manner.

3.2.1   Designing the research instrument

I used in-depth, semi-structured, face-to-face interviews as my main research instrument. I was informed and encouraged in this approach by others (Coleman, 2011, Elliott and Stead, 2009) who have recently conducted in-depth interviews with women at the top of organisations in order to:

> Contribute to the development of more in-depth understandings of women's leadership we explore in more detail how leading women negotiate and navigate their leadership 'route'. That is, how women become and sustain their role as leaders including the public and private resources they access for support. To us, this suggested the need for a method of inquiry that encourages women leaders to reflect on and make sense of their experience as a first step in working towards a more contextual awareness of the nature and learning of leadership... this chapter draws upon in-depth interviews of two to three hours each with nine women leaders from a range of settings.
>
> (Elliott and Stead, 2009) (p:65)

I approached 22 women (including my pilot participants) and interviewed all the women who agreed to my request (18 in total), and, in the main, the interviews lasted about 75 minutes, occasionally longer and once or twice much shorter. I consulted colleagues at Lancaster University about their research methods and learned from them their interpretation of the technicalities involved when interviewing senior women leaders. Building upon this and other recent senior women interview research (Coleman, 2011) and my own experience from many years of working with senior leaders, I decided to approach each participant personally, in a professional and appropriate manner, and beforehand I raised the profile of my research project to some extent so that my approach may not have come as a surprise.

I expected that I would have to negotiate with vice chancellors' 'gatekeepers', their professional assistants (PAs), when seeking their agreement to be interviewed. This relationship became a key to my success with accessibility. Whereas to begin with some of my department colleagues had been concerned about me not gaining access to women at the top, overall I was welcomed by them all, besides a couple who declined outright for specific reasons. I put this success down to a numbers of factors, not least the way I approached the gatekeepers and liaised with them throughout, thanking them at every stage for their help with enabling the interview to happen smoothly and dealing with all the local logistics. I volunteered to travel to each participant's institution to conduct the interview and asked the PA to plan the location of the interview, simply requesting privacy as I had always presumed the interview would take place in their office which would offer a private and uninterrupted space. It was essential that I fitted in with their calendar and was as flexible as possible when making appointments. I planned my interviews within a seven-month timeframe which was another reason for my access success – the gatekeepers had a long time during which to diary an appointment within their very busy schedule. This helped them to help me.

However, as I could be conducting one interview every week for a concentrated period of time, it was also important that my participants took the interviews seriously and did not cancel or postpone them unless absolutely necessary. I was pleasantly surprised that this did not happen, apart from one occasion which was unavoidable. Also, I was hardly ever kept waiting beyond the appointment time and I was particularly impressed about this as it demonstrated to me that they had taken my work seriously and were treating me professionally too. I wrote to each participant beforehand explaining: the background of my research; the value of their involvement; how they would benefit from the research; my research questions; the interview questions; their consent and its implications; a proposed interview schedule; the use of audio recording equipment in the interview; and the amount of time I would be needing from them.

3.2.2   Interview schedule

I designed the interview schedule in an organic way for a number of reasons. First, I was aware that I was potentially trying to cover a lot of ground with women who may have never been interviewed for this type of study before. Second, my questions represented signposts for both myself and my participants. Third, I wanted to be able to demonstrate how the literature had informed my thinking and consequently my questions should this conversation arise; and it would be easy to navigate around the questions in any particular order if necessary. And last, I was aware of the seniority of my participants and the type of approach most suitable (Walford, 2011, Coleman, 2012a). Fundamentally, I was mindful about the number of questions, seven, possibly being too great for a semi-structured interview and this was one aspect I considered in my pilot study, although I needed enough stimulating research questions to give the opportunity for my interviewees to reflect on their leadership past (their public and private spaces) and talk positively about their experiences in academic leadership, whilst at the same time identifying a vision for making change.

Ultimately, I am an experienced interviewer and consider that I navigated the interviews professionally. I put together a semi-structured interview schedule, by basing the questions on what I was hoping to find out about my research questions, but on the whole I encouraged the interviewee to shape the conversation. Constructionism talks about the democratisation of the research relationship, where the researcher and the researched are creating meaning together. In other words, meaning is not out there waiting to be discovered, rather it is brought into being in the process of social exchange. I am confident that this is what happened during my fieldwork and that this is why qualitative interviewing is a popular method in constructionist research methodology, with critical discourse analysis awareness an essential aspect of the researcher's reflexivity.

3.3   Analysis

The purpose of analysing my data was to record, explore and understand my participants' lived experience from their own perspective, whilst at the same time capturing aspects of their experience which are pertinent to my research questions. Data analysis is the stage of fieldwork where the real work happens and where there is a danger of contamination of the research method (Miles and Huberman, 1994). So I planned to conduct, on average, three interviews per month and my project plan built in plenty of time for the transcription and initial analysis after each one because it is vital this stage of the process is allocated enough time and energy: otherwise the interview can be undervalued.

I transcribed the interviews myself in full and agree that the analysis begins with the transcription so the time dedicated to this process is well spent (Langdridge and Hagger-Johnson, 2009). I then used the data analysis package ATLAS ti to help me code and analyse my data. My initial codings were of course guided by my research questions, but then I looked for themes as they emerged during the analysis process. Ultimately the transcript codings have structured my data analysis and informed my research findings, hence choosing these codings wisely was imperative. In addition to evidence from the interviews, I also had other forms of evidence to code and analyse. This evidence included: contextual evidence; conference papers from events I have attended during my research; quantitative data about UK higher education institutions and informal conversations.

I finished up with 89 codes and I organised and categorised these into five families which were linked to my research questions. For example: families called 'career history' and 'leadership development' and codes 'fitting in' and 'promotion processes and practices'. Ultimately, this made it much easier for me to think about my data in a way that added value to my research questions. In this way I was practising 'the science' and 'the art' of qualitative data analysis where the scientific part is systematic, analytical, rigorous, disciplined and critical in perspective and the artistic part is exploring, playful, metaphorical, insightful and creative (Patton, 2002).

Throughout the data analysis chapters I have illustrated my propositions with examples of quotations from interview transcriptions because:

> We believe the direct quotes shed critical light on the culturally patterned behaviours of the executive women and men participants and the shifting constructions of gendered power relations and practices within their institutions.
>
> (Chesterman and Ross-Smith, 2006)

I also conceptualised my three overriding themes from the coding family's data and these themes are 'headlines' for the interpretation of my data. These themes are broken down into further interpretations about how my participants:

(The negotiation and navigation of higher education gendered leadership cultures)

- negotiated and navigated 'gendered leadership cultures', often by 'fitting in' and finding their leadership voice upon becoming vice chancellor

(Higher education leadership as communities of practice of masculinities)

- experienced leadership performances in others, both male and female colleagues, which they defined as 'masculinities' which although often unimpressive go unchallenged, and have also witnessed and practised alternative, more effective, 'femininities' leadership
- observed that men attract much more sponsorship and support from those in seniority compared with that received by women, and that sponsorship and support is essential for maintaining communities of practice of masculinities

(Achieving a critical mass of women at the top)

- have strong views about the need for more women, a critical mass, in senior leadership roles and about the positive impact more women will have upon the sector
- benefited by far the most, in career development terms, from mentoring and networking (both within and out with the sector) and are ambivalent about women-only leadership education
- say they have never given serious consideration to planning their career at any stage and that they do not see themselves as ambitious
- have a complex and diverse private space which impacts upon their academic careers
- learned 'confidence' and 'resilience' and identified these as the key traits needed for success

3.3.1   Trustworthiness

I am interpreting 'trustworthiness' as a neat justification for the reliability and validity of qualitative social science (Marshall and Rossman, 2011). Unlike quantitative research methods, which seemingly offer more opportunity for robust scrutiny of results (despite the saying 'there are three kinds of lies: lies, damn lies and statistics'), qualitative methods are by their very nature unrepeatable. In other words, each of my interviews is unique and although I worked hard to plan and prepare for my meetings with my participants I could not have predicted how the conversation would go.

Obviously I used my interview schedule but this will never be a guarantee of consistency in interpersonal methods. Nor should it matter. The richness of the interview data came because each interview was different, not despite it, and this in itself signifies the validity of the data. For example, one interview took a long time to 'warm up', in fact the vice chancellor began by telling me she was on a very tight timeframe that day. Then her answer to my opening enquiry about her background seemed to go on forever. I was in a quandary, given time constraints, but let her continue in her own time. I was actually interested in her background of course but there are always more pressing things to discuss. As it turned out I now reflect that this became one of the most illuminating interviews I conducted and one of those special memories from my fieldwork culminating in extremely rich data. And the interview overran by quite some time, which was obviously her choice and in her gift, and I interpreted this as her enjoying the conversation and finding the process valuable. Of course, I never asked her so I may have interpreted this incorrectly and she may have had this agenda all along, but in qualitative interviewing the researcher has to trust herself to lead the process in a professional manner with integrity so that she can justify the 'trustworthiness' of her data throughout.

Another time I noted in my research diary how I distinctly felt a different relationship emerging than that of interviewer/interviewee. A debate had begun between us and because we were sitting at the vice chancellor's boardroom table it was like a business meeting to discuss the issues for higher education around the underrepresentation of women at the top. This was the time when I had challenged the vice chancellor several times about her views that things are getting better over time. There was something happening in that conversation that enabled us both to go to a place which had not existed in my previous meetings. A place where neither of us had a script and neither one of us was 'in control' of the knowledge production.

Unfortunately, there are issues here too. What if I am identifying too much with my interviewee? Will this contaminate my data? Contrary to the power relationship between researcher and researched that I discussed above, there is a similar issue arising from seeing yourself too closely reflected back by your participant. Reay argues that:

> There is a thin dividing line between the understandings which similar experiences of respondents bring to the research process and the element of exploitation implicit in mixing up one's own personal history with those of women whose experience of the same class is very different. Identification can result in a denial of the power feminist researcher's exercise in the selection and interpretation of data.
>
> (Reay, 1996) (p:57)

The women with whom I created my fieldwork knowledge have at the same time different but similar intersectional identities. And these mirror mine to a certain extent – generation, colour, ethnicity, educational background, class. I am, therefore, forever questioning how much I have been 'mixing up my own personal history' with that of my interviewees and how much this mixing up process has influenced 'the selection and interpretation' of the data. I am also mindful of not generalising about what the data generated from a very small number of interviews says about higher education overall. Obviously I am selecting and interpreting my data analysis in order to explore all aspects of my research questions and theoretical framework but ultimately I accept that this analysis should not become a generalisation.

3.3.2   Ethics

There are local, national and international guidelines about research ethics that informed my position on satisfying ethical protocol whilst conducting my research and there is much written about ethics and politics in qualitative research (Denzin and Lincoln, 2008, Mauthner, 2002) which I discovered and learned about as ethical considerations for my research method. I see ethics as an unfinished task as I consider ethics as a job never done. Nevertheless, my research was subject to the university's research ethics code of practice. The code involved me, my supervisor, my department, my faculty and the University Research Ethics Committee being satisfied that my methodology did not contravene the code in any way. Given that I was researching under the auspices of 'educational research' I was also cognisant of the British Educational Research Association (BERA) code of conduct for ethical research which was revised recently and can be found on their website (BERA, 2011). BERA considers that all research should be conducted within an ethic of respect for: the person, knowledge, democratic values, the quality of educational research and academic freedom.

Taking all these layers of advice and guidance into account I felt it was most important for me to cultivate my own research ethic and integrity. I do not see feminist research ethics as a box ticking exercise, which unfortunately the university's code of practice can become, nor do I see ethics as an add-on consideration that can be 'done' before the fieldwork starts. Instead ethics should permeate the value system of researchers so much so that working ethically is synonymous with research activity. This ethical behaviour encourages 'care' and 'connection' so that 'women can become visible as subjects of and in ethics' (Ahmed, 1999) and this visibility of my participants follows in the data analysis chapters. Hence:

> The ideal observer who positions others as general rather than concrete is gendered in a variety of ways. This gendering takes place through the replication of a social value attached to masculinity, the capacity to separate oneself from one's situation. But it also participates in the Cartesian separation of the faculty of reason from the extrinsic details of the body, affectivity and sociality – all values associated (negatively) with the feminine. The deployment of this masculine ideal may exclude from ethical consideration the very value of femininity with its constitutive basis in a notion of affective connection with others. In this sense, a feminist critique of a universalist ethical paradigm may actually align itself with the values associated with the feminine, not as that which women simply are, but as that which is made invisible by the universalist criteria implicit in the ideal observer. Feminist ethics may help here to expose how ethics involves fluid and contingent relationships between subjects and bodies (rather than an abstract itself). Such an ethics may employ values such as 'care' and 'connection' precisely to dislodge the universalist language of past ethical paradigms in order that women can become visible as subjects of and in ethics.
>
> (Ahmed, 1999) (p:53)

These 'fluid and contingent relationships' question confidentiality and anonymity and whether I could or could not promise these to my participants even if they were desirable. Often the concepts are used interchangeably but they are not the same thing although the concepts are closely related 'anonymity is a vehicle by which confidentiality is operationalised' (Wiles et al., 2006). I have not changed the characteristics of my participants to preserve their anonymity as this may have distorted the data albeit unintentionally. I have labelled the quotations I use with numbers, 1–18, and these numbers relate to a particular interview. There is no further information about that participant or about their institution. I transcribed all the interviews myself therefore no one else has been involved in the data analysis to break confidences. I am aware though of the possibility of a participant being identifiable from something I may say by accident during dissemination of my research and I am working hard to ensure that this does not happen. There are so few women vice chancellors that any information I may disclose about them besides the interview number (1–18) could easily lead to their identification. Not that I am overly happy with the numbering of quotations either as assigning pseudonyms always seems so much 'warmer' and in the spirit of qualitative research. Interestingly, I asked both my pilot participants about confidentiality and anonymity and neither of them were particularly concerned about these issues. One of them even reassured me that no woman at this senior level will say anything to anyone in a recorded forum that they would not repeat elsewhere, and they were sure that women of their position have trained themselves not to reveal anything that cannot be repeated elsewhere either.

However, throughout my data collection and data analysis I worked with the principles of confidentiality and anonymity being paramount. As such I am confident that the way that I have numbered my interviews and only refer to these numbers in any quotes I use has worked for this purpose. I also reassured myself that any of the quotations I have used throughout the book from any one particular interview (number) could not be pieced together to paint a picture of whom that participant must be.

Ethically, postmodern feminists are concerned about the power hierarchy that may exist when women researchers are interviewing women participants. Maynard says:

> Feminists have been critical of the ways in which sociological research involves hierarchical power relationships. Even non-scheduled interviewing and ethnographic methods can entail a deliberate separation of the researcher from the 'subject' of the researched ... feminists have rejected the inevitability of such a power hierarchy between researcher and researched. Instead they have argued for the significance of a genuine, rather than an instrumental rapport between them. This, it has been claimed, encourages a non-exploitative relationship, where the person being studied is not

treated simply as a source of data. Research becomes a means of sharing information and rather than being seen as a source of bias, the personal involvement of the interviewer is an important element in establishing trust and thus obtaining good quality information.

(Maynard and Purvis, 1994) (pp:15–16)

I am hopeful that the nature of my 'studying up' project, together with my methodology helped ensure that this 'hierarchical power relationship' did not arise and that there was space for a genuine rapport.

In summary, in this chapter I have discussed my methodological journeys and explored the key influences and considerations that have helped to shape my research in general and this study in particular. The following three chapters turn to exploring the data generated during my PhD research study, in particular through the 18 interviews with senior women leading higher education institutions. These three chapters are organised around the three key themes which emerged during my analysis of the data and which were introduced in the first chapter of the book.

4
Negotiating and Navigating Higher Education Gendered Leadership Cultures

4.1 Their lived experiences

This chapter explores the lived experiences of women vice chancellors in terms of negotiating and navigating higher education gendered leadership cultures which we know are alive and well. Gendered leadership cultures are alive and well within higher education (Acker, 2010, Bagilhole, 2007, O'Connor, 2011). Not only that, so many people are studying the culture of higher education through a gender lens that it is surprising there is anything new to research (Morley, 2013b). Should we, once and for all, not only admit that the cultures are flawed but also work together to do something meaningful to address this damaging issue? Gendered leadership culture is the glue that holds academe together through its pores and mores (Benschop and Brouns, 2003), and it was common to find my participants talking about this:

> When you are group of leaders together leading a university there's a fair amount of banter and social stuff that's going on and that's severely gendered, endless football and cricket discussions, partly I'm not interested in sport but they are male sports I can't imagine them getting excited about women's hockey or something, there's a lot of being comfortable with each other that's to do with gender, that's not leadership but it's part of bonding as a team that maybe you have to find ways that you can interact with them on a social level, to make the leadership bit work well rather than make yourself always look slightly odd. (1)

Here my participant is making a clear connection between gendered bonding and successful leadership. She feels that a component of effective leadership, in other words 'to make the leadership bit work well' is 'being comfortable with each other' and that this feeling of comfortableness is fundamentally 'severely' gendered, fuelled by the 'banter and social stuff'. She herself is not interested in sport, not that this would matter anyway because 'they are all male sports' and she 'can't imagine them getting excited about women's hockey' with the emphasis on 'them' which I interpreted as her peer group of leaders who constitute this leadership community of practice of masculinities. More importantly, as I cover in my theme on higher education leadership communities of practice of masculinities in the next chapter, it is incumbent upon her as a woman, 'the other', to find ways to 'interact with them' or, as I am interpreting throughout these data analysis chapters, to fit in. She clearly understands the implications for her if she doesn't 'find ways to interact with them on a social level' and that is that she will make herself 'always look slightly odd'. This senior woman leader in higher education is always aware of the efforts she is making to fit into leadership communities of practice of masculinities and equally well aware of the consequences for her if she does not do that gendering identity work. This negotiation and navigation of higher education gendered leadership has been discussed fully in my review of the literature above involving many commentators (Hoskins, 2010, Francis, 1999, 2010, Doherty and Manfredi, 2006) who all agree that:

> The culture of the gendered male academy is also still alive and well, with the women measuring their responses, identities and styles against the dominant male model and operating framework of management.
>
> (Doherty and Manfredi, 2006) (p:21)

The gender neutral myth in higher education belies the emotional labour women are performing throughout their leadership lives (Fitzgerald, 2013). My interviewees often referred to gendered cultures 'playing out' in numerous ways, most likely in the emotional work women are performing. For example:

> So there are different ways in which they play out. Especially at pro vice chancellor and vice chancellor levels it's quite male. Like in the actual ways that you have to perform. You can choose to do that or you can choose not to do that, you make your own choices. But I see a number of women trying to be like men. Playing their games, laughing alongside things which I know they don't agree with. Then

sometimes people think you are a bit odd or you are difficult or whatever. (16)

At the top 'it's quite male' which as she says means 'in the actual ways that you have to perform' which I am interpreting as satisfying the 'negotiation of meaning' for leadership communities of practice of masculinities which I explored fully in Chapter 2. Although, it appears she is taking an agentic approach to women when she says 'you can choose to do that or you can choose not to do that, you make your own choices'. Perhaps she doesn't actually mean the women are making a conscious choice, as Butler says too, but that when they are doing gender and having gender done to them in these leadership circles this is the result (Butler, 2006). So in her experience 'women are trying to be like men' again sounding essentialist as whether she means all men or certain types of men is unclear but by so doing women 'are playing their games' and 'laughing alongside things which I know they don't agree with'. Fitting in, in my shorthand, because she is fully aware of the consequences for women when they don't do this when she says 'people think you are a bit odd or you are difficult'. So even within these first two quotations both my participants are well aware that the penalty for not working at 'fitting in' is that they will come across as odd. My interpretation is that they are experiencing a tension between doing gender in a way that enables them to fit in or doing gender and having gender done to them as 'the other' for leadership communities of practice of masculinities.

So gendered leadership culture ultimately means that gendered power relations work to the disadvantage of femininities to such an extent that any gender 'other' than the dominant and powerful form is always being compared, and comparing themselves, to this norm (Mackenzie Davey, 2008). Moreover, this dominant culture is invariably masculine and male which is why I am exploring the implications of contemporary gendered leadership cultures throughout higher education for women in my review of the literature. The women participants in this study have negotiated and navigated higher education culture for years by virtue of their success to the top of institutions and as such, I maintain, are therefore critical and valid commentators of the 'operating framework of management', the gendered leadership cultures. These gendered cultures permeate through the processes and practices of the institution, regardless of the equality policies (Knights and Murray, 1994). Equalities policies abound across higher education as public testament to the extent of the sector's compliance with equalities legislation

(Leeds, 2013). Nevertheless masculine models and approaches to leadership thrive and this substantially accounts for the missing women at the top (Brooks and Mackinnon, 2001, Rice, 2014) despite the increasing visibility of women, possibly as a result of new managerialism which has promoted many women to middle management roles (Deem, 2007, Doherty and Manfredi, 2010). Seemingly gender neutral human resource procedures and practices, such as promotion and progression (Van den Brink, 2011, Bird, 2011, Ibarra et al., 2010), reinforce a masculine hegemony, undermine diversity and perpetuate bias against female leaders (Elsesser and Lever, 2011, Eagly and Johannesen-Schmidt, 2001, Jacobs and Schain, 2009). I heard many examples of the concern women at the top have in this regard:

> That you have fair processes, that you look at the data. I make my internal academic promotions committee every year look at the data of not only where they are but the salary. Are the women at the bottom of the salary scale? What a surprise and we know that person is really good so why is she at the bottom? Once you point it out I don't think people are negative they don't realise it's happening. (12)

> But women need to have better skills at negotiating contracts of employment. Women tend to be promoted to the first point in the pay spine. Not here because we always talk about the value and what is the value. But I bet if you look at salaries women are paid a lot less. Definitely. The policies are irrelevant. It's what is actually happening, the practices and processes that are important. (14)

> Women never get tapped on the shoulder. Quite often I've been on committees where the Chair is resigning and they have been looking for a new Chair and they will look around the table and just look at a woman as though they are invisible when they are looking for a new Chair. (15)

These women are clearly illustrating the bias that still exists in higher education despite the rigorous equality regimes. Basically they are all saying that you have to scratch the surface and examine what is actually happening in practice rather than take the policies at face value. Not only have they suffered from this gender bias themselves, they are also regularly finding gendered practices and processes in operation within their own institutions which go overlooked unless action is taken to uncover them. This is where, without naming it as such, my interviewees recognised the absolutely vital intervention of gender

mainstreaming. As one generously says 'I don't think people are negative they just don't realise it's happening' (12) which may or may not
be the case. Some less generous observers might argue that bias is never
completely unconscious and that it is within the vested interest of the
'calculus of interests...in a gender order where men are advantaged
and women are disadvantaged' (Connell, 1987) (p:285). Another confirms 'the policies are irrelevant...it's what is actually happening, the
practices and processes that are important' (14) and places the responsibility for this on women by saying 'women need to have better skills
at negotiating contracts of employment' (14) which alludes to the literature around 'the woman's problem' or rather the responsibility women
should accept for their own disadvantage. So who's to blame when
'women never get tapped on the shoulder' or when they 'just look
at a woman as though they are invisible' (15)? Between these three
quotations there is a combination of observations and solutions which
together range through 'fixing the women' to 'fixing the organisation'
to 'fixing the knowledge'.

I have interpreted from my analyses of the interview data that women
in senior higher education leadership are very aware of higher education
gendered leadership cultures such that they must take positive action
to overcome these otherwise they will continue to survive and flourish (Machado-Taylor and White, 2014, Morley, 2014). I talk more about
positive action in Chapter 6 although cultures and corresponding leadership are so inextricably entwined that I illustrate this with a couple of
examples here:

> I guess the decision making forums can feel gendered, do some-
> times, it depends very much whose chairing and how it's being
> managed, if you get a sort of environment in some university com-
> mittees, that where people are allowed just to sound off, that's likely
> to be more men than women, so chairing those events in a such a
> way that you remain purposeful on the topic and don't let people just
> sound off and grandstand that probably makes it less of a gendered
> environment. (2)

> I think it is an important attribute, it's wider than dress. It's the open-
> ness of cultures and the high trust cultures that I like to work with
> and I like to instil in other people so we all make mistakes, we won't
> do things right but that doesn't mean we shouldn't have a go at doing
> some of them and we should have people with a voice saying I'm not
> sure we are going in the right direction and have we thought this

through? So it's not I am God, so that ability for people to challenge and to be held accountable. I can only talk personally and I think that's what I see more gendered. (7)

In order for one vice chancellor to 'make it less of a gendered environment' she has to not 'let people just sound off' and 'that's likely to be more men than women' (2) whilst the other sees the 'I am God' attitude as 'more gendered' (7) and prefers her style of people being able 'to challenge' and 'the openness of cultures' so that her interpretation of gendered leadership cultures is much 'wider than dress' (7). I have interpreted here her making the connection between a lack of openness and trust with masculinities leadership cultures.

What the vice chancellor is referring to as 'decision making forums' (2) define the hub of leadership activity in higher education; such forums include senate, committees and management teams where decisions are made about the future of the institution and where gender is made and done (Wharton, 2012). So if these forums feel gendered to this vice chancellor who may have some agency and institutional authority to influence them, how must they feel for 'the other' who are in the main concentrated elsewhere? We know from the work of Ford that this gendered culture is overwhelming for many women (and many men of course) and that they feel powerless to act (Ford et al., 2008). The nature of a 'calculus of interests' is its ability to continuously reproduce itself because of the inertia created by this feeling of powerlessness on the part of 'the other'. And when 'the other' appear to be overcoming their powerlessness there is panic and chaos, as with the current debate around the feminisation of higher education (Leathwood and Read, 2009; Morley, 2011). Often then the leadership communities of practice of masculinities take measures to protect themselves from this chaos and reinforce their position of strength in such a way that it seems:

Very much a kind of a remoteness, a tendency to I think it would be described as bullying and perceived as being bullying, sort of top down edicts which haven't taken into account conversations in the institution about what's going to work and how people are going to feel about things. A kind of remoteness from really what's going on. Almost a fortress becomes reinforcing, and almost like a fortress where those people who are behaving like that don't want to go out because they don't want to hear any different so it reinforces the feeling on the ground about those people aren't engaging with us and don't know what's going on. (18)

This vice chancellor paints a visual picture of 'a fortress' which is reinforced through 'top down edicts' and 'bullying' which culminates in a feeling that these people are 'not engaging with us and don't know what's going on' (18) which all satisfies and illustrates my framework around higher education leadership communities of practice of masculinities whose boundaries are policed from the inside, thereby existing as decision-making forums which protect themselves from alternative approaches and silence 'the other' in turn reinforcing the gendering culture. Far from a passive promotion of the prevailing culture this vice chancellor has experienced the more bullying behaviour of remoteness. She has worked with people 'who don't want to go out because they don't want to hear any different' thereby building a fortress around themselves, the vested interest group. Again, this social activity of management based on hierarchy and power is masculine and male (Hearn, 2001).

Thus, it is within this frame of negotiating and navigating higher education gendered leadership culture where the hierarchy and power is represented by masculinities that women are experiencing 'invisibility' so much so that:

> In some settings it was always assumed that everybody senior would be male. So when they were talking about job descriptions for senior people it would be 'he will do this' and 'he will do that' and the person's not even been appointed yet. And I would say 'or she'. And that's been a theme. There is this mind set that anybody in senior leadership through deans and PVC [Pro Vice Chancellor] will be a bloke. Another thing the first half hour of every executive team on a Monday morning would be football. There was sort of bonding thing around the sports results which I sat there as a woman and never really had anything to contribute. They were all just having a friendly amicable bonding thing about things that were not about heavy duty work. (6)

For her, it went without saying that 'everyone senior would be male' (6). Bravely, though, this vice chancellor challenges this assumption by adding 'or she', although I would suggest this insertion on her part is in danger of having the counterproductive effect of 'othering' her. We know that language and discourse play an important part in reproducing the dominant culture and making 'the other' (in)visible (Stead, 2013). 'Think manager, think male' mind sets persist within

organisational culture to the extent that they pervade and pollute structure, processes and practices (Schein et al., 2006). According to this
vice chancellor, 'he' is referred to constantly and consistently. She is
frustrated that the prevailing mind set of her institution considers leadership to be male. Especially senior leadership as she says here, where
'anybody through deans and PVC will be a bloke' (6). The action she
takes to correct the discourse by interjecting 'or she' indicates her own
feeling of invisibility ironically. This invisibility is compounded in the
beginnings of the Monday meetings where 'as a woman... never really
had anything to contribute' (6) because of the exclusive 'friendly amica-
ble bonding thing' (6). Similarly, another participant expands upon her
feeling of invisibility when she says:

> In terms of women being invisible, masses of examples. I remember
> sitting round tables endlessly with all men. Whenever you make a
> point they just sort of sigh and look at the ceiling or say it's irrel-
> evant. And even when I was a pro vice chancellor I got that. I had
> to go all the way until I became vice chancellor. I was at an all male
> management team when I was pro vice chancellor. Often I would sug-
> gest something and people would just laugh at it. It may have been
> a silly idea, we all have silly ideas from time to time. But that sort
> of laughter was very gender specific in my view. Dismissing an idea
> which they wouldn't have done if another man had come up with
> the same idea. (15)

Maybe illustrating how hard it is to gain full membership of leadership
communities of practice of masculinities, this invisibility for women
in higher education leadership plays out in two ways fundamentally.
Women performing leadership can feel overlooked and sidelined by the
masculinities discourse around leadership so that 'whenever you make
a point they just sort of sigh and look at the ceiling' thereby 'dismissing
the idea which they wouldn't have done if a man had come up with
the same idea' (15) and at the same time are 'othered' (the wrong sort
of visibility) when they challenge it or contribute ideas because 'people would just laugh' (15). And this gendered and gendering culture
across higher education is perpetuated by UUK, which is made up of
the vice chancellors of UK higher education institutions and as such is
seen to represent the official 'voice' of higher education institutional
leadership. A recurring theme within my data is how uncomfortable
and invisible many women feel when navigating and negotiating UUK

communities of practice of masculinities and the gendered culture of UUK itself. For example:

> UUK, it's an old fashioned culture. Very few women there as you know. It is a command and control. All the boys go for the commit-tee roles and stick together. They are more likely than women to get the main committee roles. They are very keen to be in charge. And the effective women are slow to come forward. Because they are so outnumbered that they are very unlikely to have a major impact. (14)

Interestingly this male 'boys' culture is described as old fashioned whereas my data suggests that gendered leadership cultures in higher education are alive and well and very modern. That the boys 'stick together' and 'are more keen to be in charge' (14) illustrates well gendered leadership cultures across the sector that I have been exploring through the experiences of women at the top, a culture which is thriv-ing and which will work hard to maintain its dominance (Alvesson and Due Billing, 2009, Wicks and Bradshaw, 2002).

4.2 Summary

This chapter has discussed how well the data illustrates that women at the top are, and have been throughout their careers, negotiating and navigating higher education gendered leadership cultures by exploring my research participants' lived experiences.

5

Higher Education Leadership Communities of Practice of Masculinities

This chapter discusses how helpful the various features of communities of practice are for interpreting research participants' lived experiences of higher education gendered leadership cultures.

5.1 Practice as a source of coherence: *Acceptable leadership*

The education literature is full of examples of how certain types of leadership performed by those at the top of institutions, and the way we talk about leadership, are acceptable (Alimo-Metcalfe, 2005, Wajcman, 1998, Coleman, 2006, Saunderson, 2002). By inference, and rather more importantly by 'othering', there must be alternative leaderships that are unacceptable or at least less acceptable.

I have discussed 'othering' before and it is especially relevant here because wherever there is common practice and performance there is, by definition, 'the other'. Othering is not only about alternatives to 'mainstream' (malestream), but also about inferior and second best alternatives. 'The other' is an outlier, on the margins and not always even tolerated. 'Othering' is barely acceptable even when mainstream behaviours are absent (Butler, 2006). In a society hugely influenced by communities of practice of masculinities people practising their gender through femininities are familiar with feelings of 'othering'. The extremely disturbing treatment of Professor Beard whenever she makes a public appearance illustrates this well (Beard, 2014). Often patriarchy and misogyny transfers into the workplace where 'othering' is reinforced and reproduced by communities of practice of masculinities (Paechter, 2003b).

This reinforcing of common practice, or 'how we behave around here', is clearly a source of coherence. The women participants in my study provide a myriad of examples about acceptable leadership in higher education but most interestingly I found their openness about this to be refreshing. Often the women would indicate that they had never really considered leadership in this way before and that the interview provided them with a reflexive opportunity for themselves. I am interpreting them not having framed their experiences in this way in the past as tantamount to the whole issue of (un)conscious bias which is becoming vogue for human resources practitioners across higher education (Ross, 2008, Bielby, 2000). Still a fledging movement, this and associated work is all about surfacing stereotyping, and resulting bias, unconscious or otherwise. I am not wholly sympathetic with this work because I question the 'unconscious' claim and would rather talk about awareness raising around gender bias. Notwithstanding this, the argument is that the prevailing gendered culture of groups, communities and society is masked – so that members are not conscious or aware of the power and superiority of one gender. This lack of awareness, and consequently inadvertent gendered culture reinforcement, culminates in leadership structures, policies, processes and practices benefiting hegemonic masculinities. Arguably we are all seeing things through a particular lens and accepting that this frame of knowledge is the only way, which is why attention needs to be given to 'fixing the knowledge' as a priority (Schiebinger, 1999).

Thus, in order to explore the impact of this gender bias through the communities of practice criteria around practice as a source of coherence I am presenting some narratives generated around my theme of acceptable leadership:

> So certainly proper bullying behaviour I have witnessed more from men than from women. Just them being louder, talking more, dominating more, whether it's round the board table or any kind of meeting men tend to be more assertive and more confident about what they are saying and they express what they are saying in a different way as well. Women use words like, perhaps, potentially, like, might, wish, but the sayings, the verbs and adjectives for men are different ones. The language they use is different. (13)

This comment begins with a startling observation about 'proper bullying behaviour'. I am wondering what exactly is proper bullying behaviour. Is there such a thing as improper bullying behaviour? Or is the implication that bullying behaviour is normal whereas proper bullying behaviour is memorable? I have interpreted this as the vice chancellor making excuses for not challenging bullying that goes unchallenged most of the time, the improper bullying behaviour perhaps. This is why it is startling because rather like 'low level' sexual harassment and everyday sexism, this type of bullying should never be acceptable but prevailing masculinities encourages this to happen (Bates, 2014). Nevertheless, however she is defining it, proper bullying behaviour is practiced more by men than women in her experience. Then she gives a definition of what this behaviour constitutes – 'being louder, talking more, and dominating more' (13). Time and again I have heard from my participants that it appears acceptable to most people for men to dominate the conversation at all levels. This finding is supported by recent research on women and men's contributions in meetings and on the media (Martinson, 2012). I explore confidence further in the next chapter, but it's interesting in this context that bullying behaviour is connected with, from this vice chancellor's perspective as, among other things, being more confident.

Admittedly my participants are generalising and essentialising when they suggest that women are less assertive and confident because they use apologetic language often. Words like 'perhaps, potentially, like might, wish' for example. One of the other vice chancellors actually raises the issue of language with women she mentors because as she says 'stop apologising for your ideas and opinions, people are not impressed by language that seems to reflect uncertainty, and being unsure of yourself' (16). On the other hand, 'the sayings, the verbs and adjectives for men are different, the language they use is different' (13). This is relevant because according to poststructural feminist ontology, language creates discourse and discourse shapes culture (Ross-Smith and Kornberger, 2004). Therefore, whilst I am using structuralism pragmatically I am also mindful of how all leadership is made and done in the moment. So an aspect of acceptable leadership as a source of coherence for communities of practice of masculinities is about the language and theatre of leadership. One of my participants considered this in our conversation:

> I think leadership is defined by powerful leadership, it's if you look at the words you use to describe leaders they tend to be male words and sometimes they put in the odd thing about nurturing and engaging people, that's a girly one. Things like that. They tend to be male in that sense. Actually the way that the leadership club works tends to be like that, a club. Let's have a beer. Let's meet for breakfast. That's all the constructs about meetings. You go to meetings and you have

to stand from the floor and orate. That's a very male thing, rather than sitting down and having a discussion. (16)

The way we talk about leadership, according to this vice chancellor, by using male, masculine words and constructs in itself helps to define acceptable (and conversely less acceptable) leadership. Again there is a danger that she is essentialising here because all men cannot be described by these words and some women can, although I do not think that this was her intention. She does, however, see leadership as 'a club' so much so that belonging to the club means meeting for breakfast, having a beer and standing up to orate. Interestingly she goes on to talk about the attempts she is making in her institution to try another way of communicating with staff. For example, there are open gatherings in communal social spaces, such as refectories or coffee lounges, where she moves around small groups who have gathered to unwind and simply joins in their discussions. Often what is meant by the men who are being louder and talking more is actually that they are repeating themselves regularly. This was mentioned by several of my participants as being rather irritating acceptable leadership:

> I have a bit of a thing about that, I think a lot of male leaders repeat themselves and use up air time, this is a bit tricky, and I think that there is a danger for women if they do that because women who take up air time will be seen to be taking up air time and men are not seen to be taking up air time so women can't behave like that because it's not seen the same way. (1)

Firstly, she has 'a thing about it' and it has obviously irritated her for some time now but I did not get any impression that she had ever challenged anyone, man or woman, who had repeated themselves often. So leadership that is done and performed this way is what many leaders appear to suffer and put up with. This lack of challenge, for whatever reason, is what reinforces the doing of masculinities leadership as acceptable. This is also how acceptable leadership, however unacceptable this might actually be as far diversity and gender representation goes, becomes the 'source of coherence' in leadership communities of practice of masculinities. Higher education leadership communities of practice of masculinities flourish because there is something powerful about doing leadership through masculinities that resists challenge and that intimidates alternatives.

This resistance to alternatives is hard to explain except for the 'that's not how we do things around here' culture which permeates to the core of the coherence of practice fundamental to communities of practice (of masculinities) and:

> It might be a male culture but there are certain things you cannot do at work. Losing emotional control you cannot do. It's a sort of no no. I'd have to behave to men's [rules], you could just could not cry or something like that. You cannot lose control. (10)

So ultimately 'there are certain things you cannot do at work'. I am not sure here if the vice chancellor is resigned that regardless of the male culture 'it might be a male culture', there are unacceptable 'things you cannot do at work' (10). However, I would question what agency she has and how much she is being complicit here, thinking back to Foucault's power and resistance model which suggests that power is everywhere and nowhere and that power and resistance are relational. Nevertheless, I maintain that *because* it is a 'male culture' framed within leadership communities of practice of masculinities there are certain things she 'cannot do'. As I have already discussed, throughout the review of the literature above, gendered leadership cultures are the glue that holds higher education together and it is masculinities' emotionality and irrationality that is acceptable (Mackenzie Davey, 2008). Such things as game playing, back stabbing and ingratiation are acceptable to leadership communities of masculinities so as she says 'I'd have to behave to men's...I could not cry'. Although what she does not say is that maybe she could perform other acceptable, masculinities leadership emotions such as game playing and back stabbing. Not that this is probably the case anyway because women are back in that double bind of being 'damned if they do and damned if they don't' (Fitzgerald, 2013). Emulating masculinities leadership will not necessarily gain women full membership of leadership communities of practice of masculinities as suddenly this leadership performance often becomes unacceptable when performed by many women (Mackenzie Davey, 2008). Therefore, within this gendered culture, a male culture, 'loosing emotional control' you absolutely cannot do. Although 'emotional control' appears to be defined only as crying, which given we have already heard from one vice chancellor's perspective about how acceptable it is to lose emotional control by being loud and angry then, there is seemingly a bias against femininities emotions. The strong statement of 'you cannot lose control' is much more complex than first appears. Thus:

> Work in this tradition has suggested that the barriers women face in universities include those related to male definitions of merit; a 'chilly' organisational culture premised on male life styles and priorities; a culture where senior positions are seen as 'posts of confidence' and are premised on 'the way masculinity is constructed as a care-less identity'.
>
> (Brooks and Mackinnon, 2001) (p:24)

Moreover, changing women's position in universities requires changes to the gendered cultures as well as other kinds of change such as 'changing men and men's position in universities and their cultures' (Hearn, 2001). For Hearn, the most important aspect is because:

> In this situation 'women's place' is defined by men and it is a subordinate one. Men [as he sees them] are 'a social category associated with hierarchy and power...Management is a social activity that is also clearly based on hierarchy and power...Academia is a social institution that is also intimately associated with hierarchy and power'.
>
> (Hearn, 2001) (p:70)

On the whole, my participants referred to in this section are weighing up my question about masculinities leadership and seriously considering how they are interpreting this playing out in their leadership circles. More often than not my participants appeared grateful for the chance to look at their experiences of leadership through a gender lens, as invariably they had not been in the habit of doing this and by ruminating in the interview they were trying things out about their experience of established practices and performances. To summarise this section, as I have already argued, the hegemonic masculinities leadership culture often goes unnoticed and unrecognised for what it is. O'Connor especially works on this by concluding:

> There is evidence to suggest that women are less likely than men to deny the importance of gender in the context of the organisational culture. This reflects Thornton's (1989:126) observation that it is essentially unrealistic to 'expect men, as the predominant institutional decision makers, to affect this revolution magnanimously

on behalf of women'. In Harris et al.'s (1998:259) study, the system is depicted as gender neutral by those who see it as 'reasonable': with male professors in particular stressing that 'there is no sex discrimination in university or academic life'. Such attitudes reflect a taken-for-granted acceptance of the status quo by those in a hegemonic position. On the other hand, those who see the culture as flawed (and women academics were the majority of these in that study) were critical of what were perceived as institutional traditions that favour middle aged men and 'people in the know' and of patterns of direct and indirect discrimination that favour men.

(O'Connor, 2011) (p:10)

5.2 Negotiation of meaning: *Defining leadership on a femininities/masculinities spectrum*

Throughout this book I have explored the spectrum of leadership spanning the range of femininities and masculinities, and accordingly I have clarified that not only men can do masculinities nor can only women do femininities. Even before I shared my theoretical framework with my participants, they were using the spectrum model to add flavour to their experiences:

He's a man although he's probably a man other people would say was on the scale of men/woman he would be more on the woman's side, there would be more manly men than him. (1)

Meaning some people, like a lot of men, where there's 'I'm the man in charge'. I hate stereotypes but I'm talking about a spectrum. (6)

'There would be more manly men than him' is such an illuminating comment particularly if the tone of the comment is derogatory (I did not follow this up and with hindsight should have although certainly her tone on the recording sounds so). It was our shared interpretation that being 'more manly' is better than being less so that and 'on the scale of men/women he would be more on the woman's side' (1) is seemingly not preferable for any man. There was a clear negotiation of meaning happening in this conversation where it was presumed that I would share her understanding of 'manly man' and 'more on the woman's side'. And I clearly did go along with these meanings by not seeking further clarification or explanation. This has been one of the most disturbing aspects of my research for me as the researcher. That

I am possibly working with the same gender bias, lack of awareness and cultural identities as my fieldwork participants and so I may be as prone to generalising and stereotyping as anyone else. Consequently, I am able to interpret the meaning of 'emotional antennae' and 'several balls in the air' from this following comment. Again this is a relative statement, comparing women's capabilities with those of men and requiring a spectrum construct. Since sharing language and meaning is an essential aspect of communities of practice, I am reassured that this aspect of my theoretical framework is viable. So this vice chancellor observes:

> I guess, I think women bring a dimension which is something to do with emotional antennae which I'm not convinced men have, so a sensitivity to how will that be for people. A sensitivity to how will that be seen... so it's that sort of extraterrestrial emotional intelligence that we bring. I think women can balance several things at once so that we are not really phased by having several balls in the air at one time and I actually think quite a lot of the men are. (7)

Altogether these vice chancellors found it straightforward to discuss effective and not so effective leadership by using the spectrum model to help them negotiate their meaning of masculinities (and femininities) as leadership communities of practice. They also used the spectrum of leadership to help them negotiate their meaning around how things looked and felt different when behaviours more along the femininities dimensions are performed. This was an interesting development for me during our conversations. Almost counterintuitively the women in my study struggled with 'naming' the leadership culture of masculinities, whereas they talked freely about how femininities leadership resulted in more effective and more comfortable leadership environments. The status quo, perpetuated by 'the calculus of interest' renders people 'blind' to recognising the prevailing gendered and gendering culture as though this culture is gender neutral (Haake, 2009). Alternatively, I think it is far easier to name 'the other' because it is extraordinary and unusual, not the norm and feels different. For example:

> I suppose there are things that I do that you would say that's quite female behaviour, I try and bring people in. First thing I did here was have a whole series of open meetings for staff and I didn't realise at the time that what I was asking was so counter culture and people were running around saying what do you mean open meetings, how do we do that. It worked really well. It just seems natural to me to

do that. You go and talk to people, you go to them, you don't bring them to you. (17)

In this world, it is a problem that too few women are appearing in the academy leadership because the situations in higher education now are characterised by very high levels of ambiguity and the need for clarity around decision making. And I think women, and this is gendered, can hold equal and opposing thoughts in our heads at the same time. And that's very, very important. There are, I'm working often with men who just can't deal with ambiguity well. I can have an argument that says on the one hand this and on the other hand equal and opposing, and it gives us an agility to emerge and make the right decisions. (16)

But it was a lot different. It felt different. It was definitely more chatty. It was definitely more informal. It was also definitely crisper in terms of decision making. Much more steely. In a strange way I see men in lots of leadership teams and they wobble when it gets hard and difficult. With women they get real clarity. A real crispness in decision making which is great. We will pick up all the issues and hard bits and it's really clean. (16)

On one occasion the one man wasn't here and the senior management team meeting we had was so totally different. It was less confrontational. Men in that situation, however much they respect you or regard you will always be more confrontational and more willing to argue than to see others point or to reach compromises or so on. Even when we have a balance there is that behaviour. It's a lot better now and it's quite healthy and sometimes you need a bit of a difference there but it's very noticeably different. (15)

It's much, our meetings, there's only eight of us around the table. Very evenly balanced. Very collegial. A lot of laughter. Very straight with each other. No manipulation. No stabbing in the back once you go out the door. Everybody feels very supported. And it's absolutely in good times and bad, most especially in bad, that you have that kind of trust in each other. Now if that's a feminine style, so be it. A lot of talk in the press about the need for more women on boards of FTSE rated companies because actually it improves outcome and performance. That's an interesting finding. (14)

I think it's a good thing, because I think most women do have that softer style and I think that can be helpful. Rather than, we were having a political debate with these funders and my colleagues involved who are male are saying they've been absolutely stupid and we need to tell them. And my attitude has been no, no, no. We are getting what we want, let them get a bit of victory as well. There's no need to take prisoners on this. We are winning. And they reluctantly go OK, because they want to show them that they were wrong but there's no need and you can come out of it leaving them with their self respect as well. I think that tends to be more of a female attribute. (8)

Critically, these women vice chancellors have all given me examples of leadership communities of practice of femininities, communities in which a culture of femininities leadership looks and feels very different and which are, in their interpretation, more effective as leadership communities. That 'female behaviour' was 'counter culture' and that 'it worked really well' (17) begins the tone of this group of quotations from the data. Although she is rather essentialising when she says 'it just seemed natural for me to do that' because she was implying that it was natural because she is a woman. Furthermore, men 'just can't deal with ambiguity well' (16) according to the participant who argues that dealing with ambiguity enhances leadership with 'an agility to emerge and make the right decisions' (16). She is accepting of the fact about her claim 'and this is gendered' which is clearly essentialising but she is sure that many women have a different way of doing things and that this different way is a better one. So, according to this cohort of my participants, femininities leadership culture 'feels very different', 'it was a lot different', 'very noticeably different' and 'so totally different'. Again I heard the judgemental emphasis in these conversations on the comparative merits of both femininities leadership and masculinities leadership and these were overwhelmingly in favour of the former for getting the job done.

Interestingly these comparisons were not just around performing 'soft' femininities which make things 'more chatty' (17), 'more informal', 'less confrontational' (16), 'very collegial' but also doing femininities leadership in ways that on the spectrum might have been considered to have been in the masculinities domain, such as 'clarity around decision making', 'crispness in decision making' (15), 'much more steely' (14), 'no manipulation' and 'very straight with each other' (8). On the other hand my participants also concurred about the drawbacks of performing masculinities for leadership teams when they say such things as 'they wobble when it gets hard and difficult', 'they just

can't deal with ambiguity well', 'they will always be more confrontational', 'they are more willing to argue...than to reach a compromise'
and 'they want to show them that they were wrong'. Added to which
the gender balanced leadership team is 'very straight with each other'
with 'no manipulation' and 'no stabbing in the back once you go
out the door' so much so that 'everyone feels very supported' (14).
I'm especially interested in this finding about the comparative merits of doing leadership through femininities because of the well-worn
argument that it is all very well leadership being 'warm and cuddly'
but that this is unrealistic and nothing will get done, especially in
these challenging times of continual change. On the contrary, these
vice chancellors are praising the incisiveness of femininities leadership. This is not something we hear frequently so maybe it is a too
well-kept secret, not in the 'calculus of interests' of the hegemonic
masculinities cultures across higher education. Given that leadership
is all about creating cultures for change to happen it is likely that
those leadership communities capable of engendering these cultures
that will be the most effective. I am reminded of Alimo-Metcalfe's
transformational leadership communities here in which her exten-
sive research explored the impact of leadership practice on 'followers'
and unreservedly found that leadership behaviours within the spectrum of femininities are by far the most worthwhile (Alimo-Metcalfe,
2005). Over a number of years Alimo-Metcalfe and her team surveyed
thousands of public sector staff about the most effective leadership
practices they had experienced and using the repertory grid model
built up a framework of leadership performances which are transformational.

Notwithstanding all these examples illustrated above, I have also
interviewed women and discussed their lived experiences with vice
chancellors who found the femininities/masculinities spectrum, as a
negotiation of leadership meaning, over simplistic, hard to recognise
and not particularly helpful. For example:

> Not really something that I particularly recognised. I've tended to
> learn a lot from looking at people from all different backgrounds of all
> kinds of shapes and sizes and persuasions and genders and sometimes
> what you learn is how to do it and sometimes what you learn is how
> not to do it. I've learned both of those things from both men and
> women. Certainly looking at leadership teams I've seen those work
> in ways that where they have felt looked after and it's very inclusive
> and it's been a male leader; there are cases where people have been at

each other's throats and scrabbling up the greasy pole and it's been a female leader. (17)

I'm not sure that I would recognise the question about being a role model. There will be people who might have the same characteristics for whom the approach I take is relevant. There will be some who look at what I do and think well I would never do that that's not me at all. I don't think that's gendered. I think that's to do with personalities. There are a thousand different leadership styles. There isn't a woman's leadership style and a man's leadership style. That's awfully simplistic. (5)

It does tend to attract men into leadership positions who are much less aggressive who are much more concerned about personal circumstance just because universities lend themselves to that more. So although it's a male dominated leadership culture, it much less masculine than you might expect when you talk to people who are in parts of commerce who tell me horror stories of not being allowed to have a day off to look after their kids. If anything, some of the men are more understanding than some women here. I think it attracts a leadership that is much more sensitive. I've never heard ever any of my male colleagues saying, god she's off again having another kid, or I've got to look after the whatever or she's not here because, I never hear that. It might happen in small pockets but not amongst senior colleagues at all. (8)

It has been important for my study for me to surface these views and to consider these contraindications to my theoretical framework because I needed to take this into account when considering how well the framework helps us to understand why there are so few women vice chancellors. Especially when these participants are making comments such as: it is 'not something that I particularly recognised'; as well as 'I'm not sure that I would recognise' it; and how they have 'tended to learn a lot from looking at people from all different backgrounds and all kinds of shapes and sizes and persuasions and genders' (17); and that 'there are a thousand different leadership styles... there isn't a woman's leadership style and a man's leadership style' (5). These participants particularly have made me question my theoretical framework as being too simplistic and too essentialist and that what these women are telling me is more in tune with poststructuralism. Despite the vice chancellor who although providing me with contraindicative data still says 'so although it's a male dominated leadership culture it is much less masculine than you might expect' (8). So I am wary of generalising about my femininities/masculinities leadership spectrum concept although I still maintain that it has been a useful tool for engaging in conversation about the negotiation of meaning of leadership communities of practice and therefore it is still a relevant construct for my research. In a way, this is one of the aspects of my theoretical framework that is not wholly supported by the data and consequently illustrates why my more nuanced approach is necessary.

5.3   Operates as a boundary: *'Fitting in'*

Inevitably, we all survive as members of communities of practice by 'fitting in' because, according to the literature, these communities operate as boundaries in our lives, providing security and identity (Wenger et al., 2002). However, this security and identity is also performative; in other words we have to do something to prolong the membership that provides these (Paechter, 2006). Women at the top of higher education institutions belong to communities of practice of senior leadership and they work hard at fitting into these communities in order to maintain their membership status. So:

> One of things I do now, which I never used to have time for or wanted to be associated with, women's groups, because perhaps that was part of the fitting in bit and not wanting to be labelled as one of those awkward women. (6)

> And of course some of that is to do with whether you are Russell Group or not, the size and scale perhaps of what you are doing, how long you have been a university, but I do think it's interesting that our Russell Group universities are completely dominated by men, and for me my personal journey has been, I've moved from a mimic and behaving in a way that was going to be acceptable in a mainly male world. (7)

> I look at my own personal growth I think personally in trying to establish how I am comfortable operating. In early days it was power suit dressing time and there was a lot of emulating of what men would have done. I was not immune to that. I think nurture versus nature. You are influenced by what's going on and what you are about. (7)

> So I think there's a group going through where there is a range of masculinity. It's not just what you wear, that you have to wear a suit. It's not that. It's, the way I see it, it's by being female and entering the

room I am different. I can extenuate or reduce the differences. And that puts them at their ease. (12)

I think sometimes women think they do have to behave in this way too. Probably I find myself occasionally doing it and recognising it's not my natural way of behaving and I see it occasionally in other women. Whether it's the women that get into roles like that have a bit of male feistiness about them and they are prepared to put themselves in that position or when they are there they change their behaviour. It's about survival partly. (15)

I propose that there are several comments here which support the argument in relation to the work women vice chancellors do on 'fitting in' to leadership communities of practice of masculinities. Not wanting to be labelled 'as one of those awkward women' has been an undercurrent of my conversations, although only a handful of women vice chancellors I talked to actually used the 'f' word to describe themselves as a feminist. I sensed that this fear of being labelled has played out for the vice chancellors throughout their career. Mostly, I have interpreted that they have not wanted to be seen as gender politicians and that because they have invariably been the only woman in the room they do not want to add to that isolation by 'othering' themselves further. I have seen that these women have all been on a journey throughout their career, of fitting in, so that to a greater or lesser extent they perform as 'a mimic and behaving in a way that was going to be acceptable in a mainly male world' (7). Because 'it's about survival partly' (15) and this is why women work hard at performing to maintain their vital sense of belonging to leadership communities of practice, and why they are resigned to 'finding myself doing it and recognising it's not my natural way of behaving' (15). I should have taken this further to find out what her 'natural way of behaving' is and whether she interprets that as being because of her identity as a woman. Fundamentally, as one says, 'women think they have to behave in this way too' which I have interpreted to mean that she thinks, whether this is the case or not, that women vice chancellors have to behave such as they 'fit in' to higher education leadership communities of practice of masculinities. Even to the extent of their awareness of how their performance will impact upon the mainstream (malestream) community because 'by being female and entering the room I am different. I can extenuate or reduce the differences. And that puts them at their ease' (12). In other words, communities of practice by operating as a boundary in our lives require us to placate the full members of the community in our quest to belong and we learn to do this whilst practising 'legitimate peripheral participation' which often requires us to ingratiate ourselves with the full membership. So much so that 'in the early days it was power suit dressing time and there was a lot of emulating of what the men would have done' (7) and 'you are influenced by what's going on' which may mean that the influence of leadership communities of practice is too great to resist on the whole thereby, for example, taking for granted the reification 'that you have to wear a suit' (12). Even when women become vice chancellors, I have learned that not all of them are comfortable about promoting the issue of the underrepresentation of women or campaigning for women in higher education. Only a handful of the women vice chancellors that I interviewed have been willing to be involved in my 'research impact' activities showing me that they are still reluctant to label themselves in this way and only recently I overheard a comment where one was describing another as 'an honorary man'!

Moreover, women's role in communities of practice of senior leadership is about making the incumbents feel at ease with their presence as 'others' and on the whole they do this by fitting in with the codes of practice, the rules. Ironically though, in accordance with the theoretical framework model, this performative fitting in only reinforces the boundaries and deepens the masculinities cultures. Although, at the same time, it appears from my conversations with my participants that they feel they can at least relax their emotional fitting in workload once they reach the top:

I can be completely genuine and authentic now. I suppose it's easier the more confident that you get. I think this comes more the more senior you get. Becoming confident breeds more confidence. It's about being comfortable in your own skin. That actually you are doing a reasonable job and its worthwhile carrying on. (18)

It's not trying to pretend you are the same – you are equal but you are not the same. If we can't do it now we've got to be VC, who can. So it's giving permission. And I don't make it just a gender thing because I've got a lot of talented people of both genders. But giving permission to be themselves whilst still driving in the direction we want to go is really important. It worries me that somebody's trying to pretend that they are something they are not, you can't sustain it, it's not believable. (7)

I am struck by the relief the one vice chancellor is expressing when she says she is 'being completely authentic and genuine' now and by the other vice chancellor 'giving permission to be themselves' so as 'not to pretend they are something they are not' because I am confused by the identity work going on here. If, according to poststructural feminism, we are making and doing our gender identity all the time and that the workplace is a site of gender identity construction (Alvesson and Due Billing, 2009) then is it possible to be any other than authentic and genuine? I am suggesting that what these vice chancellors are expressing is the pressure of the 'boundary' work being exercised by leadership communities of masculinities, and that during their career to becoming vice chancellors they have been engaged in a learning process of the apprenticeship and legitimate peripheral participation stages of membership. Whereas upon becoming vice chancellors in some ways they now have the permission of the community (whether they ever attain full membership or not) to 'be comfortable in their own skin' (18) despite their ongoing experiences that often they are still working hard at 'fitting in' because, as one says, 'when they are there they change their behaviour' (15). Overall, the data I have been analysing here supports my position that higher education leadership operates as communities of practice of masculinities with regard to 'operating as a boundary' and I have given a flavour of this here when illustrating how women vice chancellors recognise, and perform their leadership influenced by, the leadership communities boundaries. This is not to say that the data comprehensively supports my theoretical framework and nor would I have anticipated this to be the case. Consequently there are other aspects of my theoretical framework that are less well supported by the analysis of the data and the implications for this are discussed accordingly. I consider a nuanced approach to contemplating the data I have generated through my conversations as important for refraining from essentialism and juxtaposing structuralism and poststructuralism.

5.4   Learning process: *Impact of performing masculinities*

Consequently, there is a huge learning process going on for many women entering leadership communities of practice of masculinities. They are faced with the double jeopardy of conforming, often by performing their gender 'in a way that was going to be acceptable in a mainly male world' and even then of having their performance interpreted as not appropriate for a them as a women because their performance contradicts the expectations of the femininities/masculinities spectrum discussed above. The very same leadership performance can be defined as aggressive on one hand or forthright on the other depending upon whom is doing it and who is interpreting it. For example:

> I don't know if it's more acceptable to be aggressive if you are a man. When I am, I expect my colleagues know me and they expect that. So no I don't think so, not particularly and there's a danger of confusion between being forthright and outspoken and being aggressive. I remember when I was younger I was accused of being of aggressive in meetings and I said, no I'm just saying what I think. (8)

> I can be very forthright and a couple of times I have been forthright. I've often worked with a load of women, you can be forthright with some women and they will be in tears. I will be bullying but a man can be saying the same thing and not. So you can be forthright as a woman and be obstructive or bullying which probably as a man would be perceived differently. (10)

> If you've been brought up in that environment and if you've had to fit in to survive which you probably have as a woman in a very male dominated environment then actually some of those behaviours you learn them. (11)

In terms of membership of leadership communities of practice being a learning process then these examples help us to understand how women vice chancellors are learning the implications of adopting masculinities leadership. There is a theme around whether bullying is gendered because as one vice chancellor says 'I can be bullying but a man can be saying the same thing and not' (10) and another around the aggressive-outspoken-forthright-assertive continuum which is particularly complicated for women to navigate. So much so that 'you can be forthright as a woman and be obstructive or bullying which probably as a man would be perceived differently' (10) and 'I was accused of being aggressive in meetings and I said no I'm just saying what I think' (8). Although, the issue of the impact of adopting masculinities presumes that these vice chancellors have a choice, an agency about how to perform their gender and this is not necessarily the case. Butler (2006) is ambivalent about 'choice' when it comes to performativity and other commentators struggle with this too in line with their poststructuralism framing (Eagly and Johannesen-Schmidt, 2001, Meyerson and Kolb, 2000). Inevitably, my theoretical framework around leadership as communities of practice of masculinities is structural in essence because of the compliance and categorisation of practice into the five areas I have been exploring in this chapter. However, one vice chancellor talked me through a very vivid example which she clearly remembered well and which appeared to be painful for her to recount. This one perspective helps me to understand that indeed leadership communities of practice are sites of learning about doing leadership gender and consequently about the impact for some women of doing masculinities. Thus:

> There have been times, when I think, when I was much younger and more junior where definitely I behaved in ways that I wasn't comfortable with. For example the most unpleasant time in my working career and it was working for somebody who wasn't allowing me to be myself in terms of the way I wanted to run something and manage something because he was a control freak basically. It was uncomfortable not being able to follow my natural instincts which I thought would have produced a better outcome and having to mould myself into a way which was partly covering my back but also making sure that I wasn't on a daily basis going to be criticised for what I was doing. But at the time when you are that person's junior you feel you have to respond to what is being asked of you by your manager. Yes I'd feel that moved me into the masculinities spectrum. I was behaving, however much I might feel inside that I am boiling over because something's not going right, it's very vivid in my imagination about how I behaved one day which I behaved really badly. I lost it with him and was really quite rude and I've only ever done that on one occasion. (18)

She realised that in order to 'not be criticised for what I was doing' she had to 'mould herself' into 'behaving in ways that I wasn't comfortable with'. And that her leadership at this time in her career moved her 'into the masculinities spectrum'. Thus, I maintain that the learning process taking place for some women when performing masculinities is hard emotional work and adds another dimension to women's leadership labour on top of the already significant burden of senior leadership more generally. Bilimoria calls this 'role confusion' and sympathises when the other (male) leaders on management teams see these women as merely representing the 'women's agenda' by 'othering' themselves one way or another (Bilimoria and Wheeler, 2000).

5.5   Local practice: *Sponsorship and support*

Some of that hard work can be relieved and constructively redirected through local practices, such as sponsorship and support. The women in my study observe that ordinarily men attract more sponsorship and support from those in seniority compared with that received by women. The reason I am including this in my findings is that sponsorship and support is essential for maintaining communities of practice of masculinities. Lave and Wenger talk about how members of communities of practice groom 'apprentices' to the community (Wenger, 1998) and I am interpreting this grooming as sponsoring and supporting apprentice, trainee, junior leaders because this is how those emerging leaders coming through their apprenticeship learn 'the rules of the game' and learn how to belong, acquiring full membership, to the community of practice. Of course, some people remain engaged in 'legitimate peripheral participation' and never attain the status of full membership. These people are, according to the data analysed through the frame of my theoretical framework, inevitably going to be mainly the women (and those men) who do not fit into leadership communities of practice of hegemonic masculinities.

So members of higher education leadership communities of practice of masculinities utilise their sponsorship and support of emerging leaders to prepare them for forthcoming membership. However, this membership is not universally available. Firstly, those emerging leaders warranting sponsorship and support will be carefully selected often because they are already demonstrating apprenticeship qualities. And secondly, even those leaders shaping up as apprentices initially may end up never fully satisfying the membership criteria of 'practice as a source of coherence', which requires embracing mutual engagement, joint enterprise and a shared repertoire of performances. As this participant explains:

> So there's something about this rather male dominated environment that says they see these pushy bright men as having more potential. Women who are perhaps not shouting so much about what they are doing, I don't know what it is, who are actually good or sometimes better at work are not being tapped on the shoulder. (11)

This vice chancellor is reflecting upon why in her experience women academics are 'not being tapped on the shoulder'. First of all, she is almost resigned to the existence of the 'rather male dominated environment' of higher education leadership. In my interpretation of her comment, this is her recognition of the existence of leadership communities of practice of masculinities. Secondly, according to her, this community of practice of masculinities sees 'pushy bright men' as 'having more potential'. Where are the bright women? Although presumably she would not have described these women as pushy too because she goes onto say that the women are not 'shouting so much about what they are doing'. In other words she is relating being pushy to shouting about your work and women do not do this as much as men. Finally, the real crux of the matter in terms of women as apprentice leaders is that they are actually 'sometimes better at work' than the men but nevertheless are still 'not being tapped on the shoulder'.

I am interested in this because of some critical research suggesting that one of the reasons for women being in a minority in senior leadership is because they do not deserve (by not being capable enough maybe) to be there (Hakim, 2011). On the contrary, it has been discussed with me many times during my research, albeit somewhat reflecting a touch of essentialism, that generally many women in senior leadership are more competent and more able than their male peers and that, therefore, if quotas are introduced to redress the gender imbalance there will be no shortage of qualified women to take up the posts.

I am reluctant to draw generalisations from this and other anecdotal incidents. However, this is how practice becomes engrained within communities in piecemeal and incremental ways. Often no one incident can be singled out as having huge influence on culture. Instead the repetition of incidents, each time reinforcing the community of practice until there is an acceptance that this is how things are done (Gatrell and Swan, 2008). Consequently, emerging leaders in higher education watch and learn how local leadership communities of practice of masculinities operate and they behave accordingly whereby:

> If you talk to women they tend not to put themselves forward for promotion. They tend to be less often encouraged to put themselves forward for promotion. I wasn't encouraged actually until very late on in my career. (14)

The outcome often for women is that not only do they 'tend not to put themselves forward for promotion' but much more importantly they are 'less often encouraged to put themselves forward for promotion'. Sponsorship and support from leadership communities of practice of masculinities seems to be passing them by. This inevitably leads to the human resources research which is finding that people recruit in their own image (Bielby, 2000). So much so that:

> Athena data says that men were more likely to be tapped on the shoulder than women and in particular going back to those CVs in the American research, men in senior lecturer posts were significantly more likely to be encouraged to apply for a professorial level promotion than women in senior lecturer posts. (11)

Athena SWAN is the nationally recognised award which recognises higher education efforts to address the underrepresentation in science, technology, engineering, mathematics and medicine (STEMM) subjects. Importantly, for scientists and technologists especially, the Athena SWAN data illustrates what this vice chancellor observes that 'men are more likely to be tapped on the shoulder than women'. This further enhances my argument that sponsorship and support by men for men is necessary for the perpetuation of higher education leadership communities of practice of masculinities. Even more worryingly, the more senior the leadership opportunity the more this is likely to happen because men were 'significantly more likely to be encouraged to apply'. The ECU data illuminates this observation too with only 21 per cent of professors being women and as this is an average figure, in some STEMM subjects it is nearer 5 per cent of professors who are women. More recently, HESA data has revealed a 'league table' of the ten institutions with the lowest percentage of women professors with just under 8 per cent being the lowest for a UK institution. Apparently, although it rarely happens for women, the impact of receiving sponsorship and support when it does happen means:

> That was my seminal moment really when somebody else said you can do this. We need to say this more to women because of the culture we live in where there isn't an expectation that women can take these roles. There needs to be more of us saying to more women that you can do it. (15)

> What really made a difference to me was someone whose opinion I trusted having faith in me. Women never get tapped on the shoulder. (16)

These vice chancellors have both received sponsorship and support at critical moments in their careers and it is clear that this encouragement is what made the difference. Especially when higher education is a culture 'where there isn't an expectation that women can take on these roles', a culture where 'women never get tapped on the shoulder' and, in fact, a culture where women are actually 'invisible' (Stead, 2013).

There is an expectation of leadership good practice that members of leadership communities of practice should encourage others to satisfy their potential for leadership, whatever form that might take. The critical nature of sponsorship and support for progression is emphasised when a vice chancellor has to admit 'that was my seminal moment really when somebody else said you can do this' (15) and 'what really made a difference to me was someone whose opinion I trusted having faith in me' (16). I wonder if it is this lack of sponsorship and support for many women is partly responsible for the underrepresentation of women at vice chancellor level and that the reason for this lack of sponsorship and support is because higher education leadership communities of practice of masculinities groom emerging leaders in their own image and ultimately, in Lave and Wenger's terms, many women are only ever practising 'legitimate peripheral participation' even when they appear to belong to these communities. For:

> I think it's to do with what governing bodies perceptions and ambitions are and what they think a traditional university is like and therefore the kind of qualities that they think are important for the leader of that institution or the senior manager of that institution and all sorts of things come into play and that's where there's tapping on the shoulder and networking. (18)

Here, another dimension to sponsorship and support is introduced by this vice chancellor. Governing bodies adopt a powerful role in terms of promoting and promulgating leadership communities of practice of masculinities in higher education as do search agencies, or head hunters as they are often called. There is a growing recognition about the conservative influence these bodies are having on the diversity of senior leadership across the sector. This was reflected in the Breakwell study (Breakwell and Tytherleigh, 2008) and has been picked up by the media recently (Grove, 2012). There have been several anecdotal experiences during my research from women within the sector either being approached by search agencies about a senior position or being on appointing panels for long/shortlists put together by search agencies which reinforce the rumours that these search agencies, working to the brief of governing bodies to a large extent, are influencing the potential diversity of higher education leadership by their selection practices. Recent research shows that 17% of PVCs appointed through search agencies are women compared with 27% through internal recruitment (Shepherd, 2015). Thereby, they are indirectly encouraging the sponsorship and support of and by higher education leadership communities of practice of masculinities.

5.6 Summary

In summary, this chapter has discussed how well leadership communities of practice of masculinities have shaped the learning of leadership for women in higher education. The following chapter turns to discuss the importance of achieving a critical mass of women for interpreting gendered leadership cultures more favourably with regard to gender equality in leadership.

6
Achieving a Critical Mass of Women at the Top

> Enough means there's a critical mass but I'm not sure where that is but so that it isn't odd. I hope I have laid the foundations for more women to be in the pipeline. (6)

My conversations with women vice chancellors invariably covered the importance of more women at the top for achieving gender equality and in this respect these conversations have reflected the ongoing conversation across sectors, beyond education, about the value of a critical mass of women for changing the status quo. Women now make up more than 20 per cent of non-executive directors on FTSE 100 boards, although the figure for women executive directors is still under 7 per cent, very slightly up on the baseline 2011 figure (Vinnicombe et al., 2014).

6.1 Tackling the status quo

Often vice chancellors reflected on their experiences throughout their careers and how they have become resigned to things being as they are, albeit changing slowly. Most of the women in my study were familiar with the isolating feeling of being the only woman in the room at senior leadership meetings:

> You will walk into a room and there will be quite a high probability you are the only woman in the room. There will be quite a high probability that a woman will be interviewed by a predominately male panel. Once you get around 30 per cent it will be easier to make sure that doesn't happen. It becomes also I think, once you have a minority of critical mass they feel confident enough to say no, to not agree,

and not feel everybody will remember them because they were the only person not wearing a grey suit in the meeting. (11)

The pool of people who are putting themselves available at the moment for senior roles is dominated by men. Why is that? It's dominated by men because they have that straightforward career stuff. They think they've got a right to do it and expect themselves to do it. And many people recruit in their own image still. So you've got that dynamic still of a community of practice. You go to UUK and most of the male VCs look very similar. (7)

I am interpreting these comments to mean that regardless of the (extremely slow) current pace of change the status quo is unacceptable and something needs to happen. In other words:

There are lots of things that we need to do. We can't just say it's an issue and that's how it is. There are too few [women] professors and therefore there will be too few vice chancellors. Again professors are in certain subjects. If you look at physics its tiny per cent, in biology it's slightly better, in the health professions it's more. But we can't draw all our next vice chancellors from the health professions. (16)

So there are 'lots of things' that need to be done. A growing sense of something needs to happen. I maintain that 'something' is creating and sustaining a critical mass of women at the top because:

Until you get to that critical mass...because then you've never walked into a room and felt you were the only woman there. Once you get to those sorts of percentages. Once it stops feeling that when the chaps go to the loo they are continuing the meeting and you are the one person stood outside the door wondering what they are talking about. (1)

Thus reinforcing the argument about leadership communities of practice being exclusive and policed from within, such that performing hegemonic masculinities marginalises 'other' performances, or by 'being female, doing gender' brings confusion and even chaos (Priola, 2007). As this vice chancellor says:

In terms of how many women, it needs to be at least a third, there's something about what's the tipping point...it's only as you get up to a third that it gets accepted and routinised. And in terms of role models it's not the token women then it's actually much more accepted. (7)

There is a general recognition too from my research participants, in sympathy with Carvalho et al. and Morley (2013, 2014), that until action is taken to redress the gender balance in leadership then the minority will always be in the minority and change will happen at a glacial pace. Achieving a critical mass of women at the top is one way that gendered leadership cultures can be deconstructed as organisations are a 'site of gender construction' (Alvesson and Billing, 2009) and attaining critical mass – going from one or two women (a few tokens) to at least three women (consistent minority) – makes it possible to enhance the level of organisational innovation and success (Torchia et al., 2011). Achieving this all-important critical mass is the seemingly insoluble conundrum of modern leadership. Wherever masculine models of leadership prevail, diversity must be manufactured and sustained (Kanter, 1977). Otherwise alternatives will always be 'other' and femininities will always suffer from the 'othering' process – tolerated but never mainstream (malestream). Research shows gender diversity will not occur across all the professions for at least 70 years (Commission, 2011), but:

> Waiting 70 plus years isn't acceptable. I think it is important to have more women at my level. (14)

Not that more women 'at my level' necessarily means more feminist women and this illustrates why the critical mass argument is so complex and nuanced as discussed more fully in Chapter 2.

6.2 The positive action dilemma

> The men wouldn't say we don't want to be there unless on merit. Clearly not all men are there on merit. (14)

Positive action is no substitute for laws which tackle direct and indirect discrimination but recognises that these are only capable of bringing about a limited amount of social change. Discriminatory attitudes are deeply embedded in society meaning that underrepresented groups suffer because of, for example: social pressures prevent discrimination coming to light; views are shaped by dominant social assumptions, stereotypes and bias; the lack of social capital of disadvantaged groups; limited participation of underrepresented groups in decision-making processes; and the lack of role models (Sprague, 2013). Consequently, discrimination, disadvantage and 'structural inequality' persist despite legislation. It is this structural inequality which positive action aims to address (O'Cinneide, 2012). Positive action describes a wide range of policies and initiatives which 'seek by means of positive steps to alter existing social practices so as to eliminate patterns of group exclusion and disadvantage' (Bell et al., 1996) (p:234) and these measures can be categorised as follows: eradicating prohibited discrimination; purposefully inclusive policies; outreach preferences; redefining merit (McCrudden, 1986). Nevertheless, there can be confusion around positive action with some people misinterpreting this as positive discrimination and it can be this confusion that causes the backlash. It is not surprising therefore that women vice chancellors find this space around positive action confusing too and a divisive issue where:

> I do believe in positive action and I do believe in quotas, I believe they concentrate the mind, I'm not sure how you could enforce a quota at VC level – its 135 different institutions it's not like a board, I think quite a lot of university boards and councils try, I mean mine here is quite good in terms of gender, rubbish at ethnicity but good in terms of gender, but I think we as women VCs could be doing more to encourage the next level down and the next level down and the next level down. (3)

> I am absolutely dead set and implacably opposed to anything that has quotas or anything else that could be read as tokenistic or anything else that takes the gloss off for people who actually have achieved by their own actions and by their own good qualities. (17)

> I think it's really difficult because all the women who have got to the position that I am in and higher positions you want to feel you have got there because you are good at your job, but we also recognise that until a few women get there and to be seen to be doing it it's going to be hard to convince people women can do it, personally I would hate to have thought I got somewhere because of quotas but that doesn't mean I think quotas are a bad thing. (1)

These vice chancellors represent the range of views of my participants who were either completely in favour of positive action, completely against it, or pretty pragmatic about the inevitability. The vice chancellor implacably in favour is so because 'they concentrate the mind' and the one definitely against is because they 'could be read as tokenistic'.

There often appears to be no room for negotiation where opinions are so polarised. Research from Stanford University explores this dilemma and found that women explain the missing women in senior roles in two ways, either by the structural processes and practices creating a 'glass ceiling' or by the meritocratic culture only rewarding women who work hard enough and by being the best person for that role (Wynn, 2012, Saunders et al., 2009). Similar to this vice chancellor:

> I'm finding it really confusing for me this space around positive action. I'm able to know that I got the job because I was the best person. (16)

Whereas those women interviewed who were relaxed about positive action could see that without doing something to manufacture change then masculinities leadership will thrive for:

> That ties back into why we need some positive action. Well actually we need to redress that imbalance, because it's not positive action, it's actually the fact that without positive action it's encouraging the men and the data saying to us is that actually the people who need encouraging is the women. So positive action is to redress what for some reason is a cultural or maybe something else, a genetic imbalance, or a mix of culture and genes and positive action is needed to redress that or otherwise we are going to miss out on the quality that we could have. (11)

This vice chancellor can see that keeping things the same is 'encouraging the men' but is also neglecting the 'quality that we could have' by not encouraging the women. This means her 'mixture of culture and genes' has resulted in masculinities leadership communities which require challenge through positive action. Positive action was often interpreted by participants as quotas. Although these can be aspirational they are often divisive and are a poor example of positive action measures (such as gender mainstreaming) which tackle the culture of masculinities producing and reproducing hegemonic patriarchal systems if left unchecked (Bickley, 2010, Tiessen, 2007, Bendl and Schmidt, 2013, Mavin and Bryans, 2002, Page, 2011). Hence, two of the vice chancellors suggested a need for something more:

> Positive action in my book is about getting the pool of people to see themselves as being perfectly capable of doing the next level of job.

The numbers here have got worse... the fact that there are far fewer women and the fact that some of the networks that used to exist have perhaps collapsed I would say there is much more of a male network in senior levels in universities but there isn't quite the same female network. (4)

What's really important is that I work with people who are really good and really committed and giving 100 per cent if not more. I haven't set out to try and increase the number of women but I do think women should have a greater opportunity to be considered and we should make the roles flexible enough so women do put themselves forward. I think women select themselves out. I like the idea of voluntary quotas because it says there's an aspiration here but I wouldn't want to be a women who got a job just because of being a women. I would want to feel I got it because I was bringing something important and slightly different. (6)

In a number of conversations during the interviews, positive action was described as implementing measures which redress the imbalance women suffer because of the preferential position men inhabit due to masculine models of leadership. Whether this means getting women 'to see themselves as being perfectly capable of doing the next level job' (4) or women having a 'greater opportunity to be considered' or making 'the roles flexible enough so women do put themselves forward' (6) and a whole myriad of actions which are not about positive discrimination but instead seek to redress the imbalance that normally occurs in the favour of many (white, middle class) men within masculinities leadership communities. From these participants' perspectives:

I think it's scandalous that there are so few [women] as I think its scandalous there are so few women MPs and so few women in lots of other senior roles. (15)

Consequently, there are positive action measures vice chancellors are taking themselves which previously made them uncomfortable perhaps as:

One of things I do now, which I never used to have time for or wanted to be associated with, women's groups, because perhaps that was part of the fitting in bit and not wanting to be labelled as one of those awkward women. That's changed now. I do talk to the women's researchers' group and I have given talks to other women only groups. Those of us who are older now should be trying to encourage people. (6)

That was my seminal moment really when somebody else said you can do this. We need to say this more to women because of the culture we live in where there isn't an expectation that women can take these roles. There needs to be more of us saying to more women that you can do it. (15)

I think it's incumbent upon all of us whether we are women leaders or not to actually think about how we can encourage more women to progress through the ranks within higher education. (18)

I see it as my responsibility to encourage and support other women, who else is going to be able to do it, I feel it's a very important responsibility. (2)

To me this suggests glimmers of change whereby women in senior leadership are taking on some of the responsibility for making sure things are different for women coming through (contrary to much of the literature about women not helping other women which I discussed at the end of Chapter 2). Perhaps because 'that was my seminal moment really' (15) or whether because 'it's incumbent upon all of us' (18) otherwise 'who else is going to be able to do it' (2) suggests that these vice chancellors have reconsidered their position on positive action in order to 'encourage more women to progress through the ranks' (18). Once again it is important to consider these comments in the context of refraining from essentialising women or generalising the benefits of positive action for all women. Critically, the importance of taking positive action in the field of gender equality is around the difference it will make for women coming through and therefore for challenging leadership communities of practice of masculinities.

6.3   What difference will it make?

I have this notion that if the sector had more women as leaders then that atmosphere would shift a bit, if not a lot. I think it would shift. To something that's more inclusive and less hostile and less, we are better than you aren't we. It's very hard to describe but very easy to feel. (18)

The difference achieving a critical mass of women in senior leadership roles will make underpins the emancipatory agenda of this research alongside the recognition that this is fundamental to changing the representation of women in leadership overall (Bickley, 2010, Butler, 2013, Kramer et al., 2006, Vinnicombe et al., 2008). Nevertheless, there have been many examples during my conversations about how gender diversity changes leadership cultures:

> I wasn't trying to appoint women I just appointed the best people for the job but we ended up with more women than men and a very different sort of environment. (15)

It is interesting that Kanter suggests 35 per cent as the minimum membership of a 'tilted group' because during my data generation several participants defined their idea of a critical mass of women at the top as being 30 to 35 per cent and that this would make a difference to the gendered cultures.

> So I feel that things have improved, with more women there, with women more in senior positions the whole atmosphere has changed for the positive. By talking about your positive examples, it will shift even more, it will be more representative of society. (13)

There is not much difference noted in dynamics when women constitute fewer than 25 per cent of a community; at 30–35 per cent there becomes a 'feeling of normality' and once representation is greater than 35 per cent a difference in decision making is noticed (McGregor, 2011). Accordingly, vice chancellors are not only experiencing this difference but also seeing that difference becoming routine and acceptable:

> Whereas with everybody you get a mix of inclinations and abilities and ambitions once you get a larger number. But it's only as you get up to a third that it gets accepted and routinised. And in terms of role models it's not the token women then it's actually much more accepted. (7)

Whereas lone women on boards are not listened to or taken seriously and may be expected to represent all women's views (Erkut et al., 2008), even two women, although demonstrating that all women are not the same, can still be treated as 'tokens' and a critical mass of three or more are needed for the board to be 'normalised' (Erkut et al., 2008). Eventually that normalisation has the potential to become the preferred alternative, no longer 'the other':

> I think it's pretty cool that there are women who lead communities of practice which are notably different and create opportunities for people instead of being, so that they are more feminine rather than more masculine communities and people need to know that is possible and that it's successful. (4)

The dual justifications for promoting a critical mass of women in business are about challenging masculine bias in beliefs about leadership and addressing group dynamics that operate in small groups (Vinnicombe et al., 2008). Without appearing to be essentialising, the loss of women results in a wastage of talent and inefficiency whereas increasing the participation rate of women in senior roles and engaging women in positions of influence brings competitive advantage. Women perceive more exclusion (chilly climate) from academic departments with a low representation of women (Maranto and Griffin, 2011). Focus on short-term business drivers and masculine cultures help to exclude women from executive roles and this has the potential to impact on organisational performance (Bickley, 2010). Ultimately, sex and gender roles are more stereotypical and more problematic in organisations with relatively low proportions of senior women (Ely, 1995), and it is not just the number of women in organisations that determine the gendered culture or otherwise. Instead it is the number of women in powerful and influential roles or as Ely calls them 'sex-integrated firms' that really makes a change to the gendered nature of organisational culture. In order to achieve this critical mass of women in more powerful and influential roles aspirational voluntary quotas could be established as:

> I like the idea of voluntary quotas because it says there's an aspiration here but I wouldn't want to be a women who got a job just because of being a women. I would want to feel I got it because I was bringing something important and slightly different. I do think it creates a different atmosphere. (6)

Thus, I have been exploring gendered leadership cultures in higher education within a theoretical framework of leadership communities of practice of masculinities and, in particular, how women thrive in these cultures and how improving the representation of women in senior leadership thereby achieving a 'critical mass' might make a difference to entrenched gendered leadership cultures even if more women does not necessarily mean more feminist women. What is interpreted as 'a critical mass' is significant for long term, sustainable change in the representation of women at the top. Without this critical mass there will only be piecemeal and incremental change, playing around at the edges and never tackling the real issue and in addition to the critical mass what matters are 'critical acts' (Chesterman and Ross-Smith, 2006). These critical acts refer to symbolic positive action interventions such as those encouraged by the Athena SWAN agenda (Forum, 2010) and which importantly do not confuse positive action with positive discrimination (O'Cinneide, 2012).

More women in leadership, at least a critical mass, changes to a 'warmer' leadership culture and widens the range of topics discussed (Erkut et al., 2008). As these participants say:

> It's a very cooperative group; it's a very collegiate group. I wonder sometimes whether it's perhaps a bit too collegiate. But it is a group of people now who do what they say they'll do. (6)

> But it was a lot different. It felt different. It was definitely more chatty. It was definitely more informal. It was also definitely crisper in terms of decision making. Much more steely. (16)

> Very evenly balanced. Very collegial. A lot of laughter. Very straight with each other. No manipulation. No stabbing in the back once you go out the door. Everybody feels very supported. And it's absolutely in good times and bad, most especially in bad, that you have that kind of trust in each other. (14)

Critically, these women vice chancellors suggest the difference more women in leadership, a critical mass, makes is twofold. Not only do the leadership cultures become more collaborative, supportive and collegial they also become more incisive and effective because of enhanced decision making and overall determination to get the job done. This is an interesting reflection because this seems to be the experience of these vice chancellors despite my concern that more women does not necessarily mean more feminist women, or more women prepared to help other women. This is yet another example of how a much more nuanced exploration of the issues is critical.

6.4   Summary

In summary, this was the final chapter discussing and interpreting the data generated through conversations with senior women leading higher education institutions. This chapter concentrated on the importance of achieving a critical mass of women in leadership may be for influencing higher education gendered leadership cultures. The following (and final) chapter moves to considering the way forward.

7
The Way Forward

This chapter builds upon the full discussion about my data analysis in the three previous chapters, draws thematic conclusions and informs my recommendations for further research.

Fundamentally, the conclusions in this chapter answer the research questions which underpinned my PhD research study. I maintain that the construct of leadership communities of practice of masculinities is meaningful within higher education gendered leadership cultures and consider this in the first two of my headlines themes below. I also maintain that achieving a critical mass of (feminist) women in higher education leadership communities of practice of masculinities is valuable for moving forward.

Overall, this chapter enhances my threefold contribution to knowledge – seeking out and engaging with the silent and strange voices of women vice chancellors; interpreting higher education gendered leadership cultures, through evidence and argument, within the theoretical framework of leadership as communities of practice of masculinities; and making the case for positive action across higher education with the aim of achieving a critical mass of women at the top – by summarising my conclusions accordingly.

7.1 Conclusions

7.1.1 The negotiation and navigation of higher education gendered leadership cultures

There is ample evidence from my data that gendered leadership cultures survive within UK higher education and Bagilhole and Morley support this in their recent works too (Bagilhole and White, 2011, Morley, 2013b). I can safely conclude, therefore, that gendered leadership culture is not a thing of the past but instead is very much alive and well. For too long it has been suggested that time will make a difference and that the gendered leadership culture of today is merely a throwback from times gone by before equality legislation was fully introduced and embedded. This is certainly not supported by my findings nor is it supported by data from other sectors. Only recently, as discussed in the introduction, in March 2013 Lady Hale argued that the judiciary needs to step down from the time served fence and accept that despite 30 years of women entering the profession in greater numbers than men there are still gendered cultures that dare not speak their name which results in women being seriously underrepresented at the Bar and in other senior posts.

This underrepresentation plays out for women in UK higher education too, providing more evidence (should any more be needed) that gendered leadership cultures are entrenched and self-perpetuating. Each year the ECU conducts quantitative research across the sector which produces data about all aspects of diversity in employment (ECU, 2014). The latest figures reinforce the lack of representation of women at all levels and in all types of leadership. Thankfully, LFHE is making leadership diversity development a key priority now (Bebbington, 2012). LFHE and ECU jointly funded a project to investigate the impact on leadership diversity of their Top Management Programme by following the careers of its alumni and it is anticipated that this project will inform a review of this influential programme (Manfredi et al., 2014). The role of the LFHE in the future of the representation of women in leadership is relevant to my research because many of the women vice chancellors that I interviewed had attended the Top Management Programme and we talked about their views of the part the programme played in their success. In 2013 the first cohort of hundreds of women joined the LFHE Aurora development programme for women (http://www.lfhe.ac.uk/en/programmes-events/you/aurora/, accessed 12 August 2014).

The overriding conclusion about gendered leadership cultures, from my data, is that women at the top of institutions across UK higher education have learned throughout their career to navigate and negotiate the gendered and gendering culture and that this negotiation and navigation is partly responsible for their success. There is so much evidence, as presented in the data analysis chapters, that women are working hard at fitting into an inhospitable culture. Admittedly, one or two of my participants did present contraindicative data and I have weighed this up alongside the confirming data in the discussion about my analysis too. Nevertheless, for the women who revealed to me their experiences of negotiating and navigating higher education gendered leadership cultures, not only are these senior women performing such emotional labour on their leadership identity, they are also sanguine about having to do so, on the whole. Very few of the women interviewed considered this unreasonable or resented their investment in negotiation and navigation, besides several of the vice chancellors declaring that life is more comfortable at the very top because at least now they can 'be themselves'. This is concerning, not only because of the energy these women are expending on fitting into gendered leadership cultures but also because of the message this gives to women (and other underrepresented groups) coming through. I conclude, therefore, that often women in higher education leadership may have an extra requirement on their job specification which involves chameleon-like features (Alimo-Metcalfe, 2010).

7.1.2 Higher education leadership as communities of practice of masculinities

Throughout the book I have appraised Paechter's theoretical framework around communities of practice of masculinities (Paechter, 2003b) and applied it tentatively as an underpinning framework for my work. On the whole I am reassured that this framework is helpful to me and therefore conclude that gendered leadership cultures in UK higher education can be interpreted as interrelated with leadership communities of practice of masculinities. I propose that the features Paechter uses to define communities of practice of masculinities are satisfied, on the whole, in the learning of leadership in higher education and that I have elaborated on her theory accordingly.

First of all, learning leadership takes place within communities of practice and as such these communities of practice have been adequately explored as sites of learning by Lave and Wenger (Lave and Wenger, 1991). On the whole, I conclude, learning leadership in higher education satisfies Wenger and Lave's communities of practice construct.

Second, learning leadership is synonymous with learning leadership gender and gendering as described by Paechter in her work on femininities and masculinities as communities of practice (Paechter, 2003a, 2003b). The extension of her framework that I propose is that hegemonic masculinities in the form of doing leadership exists in the mores and pores of higher education leadership communities of practice and, therefore, that it is inevitable when learning leadership academics are also perpetuating masculinities.

Finally, Paechter also sees communities of practice of masculinities as sites where the power knowledge nexus plays out (Paechter, 2006) and I can conclude, from the analysis of my data, that higher education leadership communities of practice of masculinities serve this purpose too. This is perhaps even more critical to the perpetuation of the hegemonic masculinities leadership cultures across the sector.

So, there is an abundance of data from the fieldwork to endorse my conclusion that leadership communities of practice of masculinities prevail and that many of the women at the top have experienced this. Again some of my data provides a contraindication to this conclusion and I have discussed the implications of this for my work in data analysis Chapter 5. Notwithstanding this, women vice chancellors invariably described how these leadership communities operate, even though the 'shared practices' are often unimpressive. In addition, they easily provided lived experiences of leadership communities of practice of femininities and how much better these can be for getting the job done.

7.1.3 Achieving a critical mass of women at the top

Throughout this book I have sought to set my research into a context of the missing women at the top across all sectors. There is a growing conversation about more women at the top, not just in higher education but across the private, public and third sectors. More often than not each day brings more media coverage of the issue in politics, the law, commerce, journalism and sport, let alone the church. Throughout these conversations the emerging discourse is around achieving a 'critical mass' of women as a prerequisite for step change (Kanter, 1977). I conclude that 'critical mass' is an emerging discourse amongst the women participants in my research, reflecting the conversation in the literature (Bickley, 2010, Butler, 2013, Kramer et al., 2006, Vinnicombe et al., 2008). There are two factors informing their thinking on this: first, that the pace of change will be so slow otherwise; and second, the positive message this will give to women coming through.

The currency of this 'critical mass' is irrefutable according to Chesterman (2006) owing to the leverage it affords culture change. Nevertheless, I concur with other commentators (Ely, 1995) who argue that it is not just numbers of women in leadership that makes the difference, it is women in posts of seniority, visibility and influence. Ideally more feminist women too. My research participants regularly used the concept of 'critical mass' without being able to quantify this. I got the sense that to them it was more symbolic than specific. Regardless, they seem to be convinced of the importance of significantly growing the women in the leadership cohort and overall I found no contraindicative data about this issue, unlike with my other two conclusions. Nevertheless, it is important to emphasise that more women will not necessarily lead to more feminist women.

What is more complex and nuanced is the means by which this critical mass is to be achieved. My conclusions here are mixed. There is real controversy about adopting positive action to achieve the desired critical mass. Interestingly, there are three standpoints from the research with each being held with passion: nearly half of my interviewees are fundamentally opposed to positive action (however they interpret that); almost the other half are in favour, albeit reluctantly; and, as explored in the data analysis Chapter 6, the remaining few are undecided and struggling with their indecision. The conclusion I draw from this is that women are polarised by this debate. One way or another, women are passionate about the implications of positive action for them and their peers and even the women who are undecided are clearly tested by their indecision, seeing it as a real dilemma.

I have changed from being ambiguous about positive action measures during the process of conducting my research and am now in favour of gender mainstreaming and positive action cultures. This has been one of the issues where I have identified closely with my participants and have been fully reflexive about this partly because of the shared intersectionalities between us of gender, class, ethnicity and generation. I am concluding that positive action in this context means a wide range of interventions addressing the 'fixing' of all three barriers to equality – 'knowledge', 'organisation' and 'women' – not simply implementing quotas. So, in terms of 'fixing the women' such things as women-only development programmes, for example. Once again, the women I interviewed were torn over this topic, as they were about women to women mentoring and the value of women leadership role models. I am left to conclude that just as my feminist epistemological position and my interpretation of my theoretical framework have resisted me seeing women as a homogeneous group so women do not see themselves as that either, or as obliged to help other women. Thus, the women in my study have more difference than similarity (and maybe this would be the same for their male counterparts too) and there is no clear evidence of sisterhood or femininities solidarity. Maybe women, in all our guises, are not presenting as leadership communities of practice of femininities with corresponding 'matriarchal dividends', sponsorship and support, and invested self-interest.

7.2 Recommendations

This section of the book builds upon my conclusions above and discusses three significant recommendations emanating from these. Given that I have been researching from an emancipatory platform these recommendations are fundamentally practice based. I use these recommendations to pursue an agenda for further work which I hope will help to initiate and consolidate change in higher education leadership. These three recommendations aim to influence policy and practice in the field and simultaneously encourage further research.

7.2.1 Recommendation one: Women-only leadership education (fixing the women)

- Women – only leadership education policy and practice across higher education are informed by a major evaluation study.

This is a critical recommendation having experienced a leadership development background in which women-only development has been frowned upon for some time. Consequently, I have not come to this decision lightly. Only by exploring this issue with my participants and by thinking about my findings in a nuanced fashion have I developed the confidence to argue the position that I now favour women-only leadership education. Consequently, I am delighted to see that Morley is advocating women-only development (Morley, 2013b). The reasons for my initial ambivalence about women-only leadership education were not dissimilar to the arguments that I had heard from my research participants. Thus, it is imperative that women-only leadership education interventions are not perceived as remedial. It is not 'the fault' of women that such interventions are necessary. Also, women should still be encouraged and given ample opportunity to join mainstream (malestream) leadership education programmes; it should not be an either/or scenario for women or their sponsors. At the same time, these mainstream programmes should be adapted to incorporate leadership diversity education rather than learning about leadership diversity being an 'add on' or stand-alone module as is often the case. Given the reluctance of many people to support women-only leadership education, I recommend that a major evaluation study is conducted to demonstrate its value to higher education.

Moreover, I suggest that such a study should build upon fledgling work (Ely et al., 2011) by evaluating the theory, design and impact of women-only leadership education programmes within the context of higher education's ambition for greater diversity at the top. This study would be rich in impact and engagement potential as there is a growing conversation in the UK around 'the missing women' at the top across political, social, cultural and economic life. Almost daily there is media coverage about the underrepresentation of women in senior leadership across the law, the church, STEMM, the police, the arts, politics, the civil service and, of course, education. Even professions in which women predominate in lower ranks there is a deficit of women making it to the top. Consequently, the outputs from such evaluation research would be easily transferable from the higher education sector into all other sectors – public, private and voluntary. Already some organisations are experimenting with women-only leadership education, although because there is insufficient evaluation and relevant data upon which to base their interventions they are often implementing their strategy with a leap of faith.

Women-only leadership education has been unpopular for a while now, having seen its heyday in the 1980s and 1990s, because the pedagogical theories have failed to keep up with practice. Either mainstream programmes were adapted for women so that the same programmes that were delivered to mainly male groups were delivered to women-only groups instead, or a 'fix the women' approach was taken to programme design which denied the frame of gendered leadership cultures within which women in leadership operate. This evaluation study would take a fresh look at the value of women-only leadership education within the context of achieving a critical mass of (feminist) women in senior leadership in contemporary higher education.

My recommendation about pursuing evaluation research is both engaging and impactful. It is also extremely timely given the mood of the UK economy for greater diversity in leadership and fairer representation of women at the top and the recent move by LFHE to launch their Aurora programme. There is emerging work on the theoretical frameworks behind the resurgence of this type of intervention (Ely et al., 2011, Clarke, 2011) but much more needs to be done so I am recommending further evaluation research to inform both policy and practice.

7.2.2   Recommendation two: Gender mainstreaming (fixing the organisation)

• Both gender mainstreaming policy and gender analysis practice are adopted comprehensively across higher education.

This is a significant policy development recommendation because of the relationship between gender mainstreaming and positive action which addresses the underrepresentation of women. Also, this recommendation about gender mainstreaming is fundamentally practice based as:

> The first step is to identify the ways in which the status quo is designed with men in mind, the second step is to open systems up to accommodate men and women equally.
>
> (Morley, 2013b) (p:12)

The gender mainstreaming movement has been spreading from development (Tiessen, 2007) across many parts of the public sector and even into higher education; also, gender analysis is at the heart of gender mainstreaming (Bendl and Schmidt, 2013, Page, 2011). Indeed, as I have explored in the data analysis discussion chapters, several of my participants gave me examples of the gender analysis practice they already undertake in their own institutions. Thankfully, the vice chancellors who were keen enough to instigate the analysis appear to also have been keen to follow this through with measures to address the issues which were highlighted in this study. Such good practice of pursuing analysis and action was one of the learning points from the keynote address at Lancaster University conference on 'the missing women in higher education leadership' in June 2013. To gain follow through, gender mainstreaming is crucial and it is imperative that action follows analysis rather than analysis being seen as a bureaucratic exercise where nothing actually changes as a result (Bendl and Schmidt, 2013, Page, 2011).

There is often 'disconnect' between an organisation's headline equality policies and processes, and the resulting embedding of practices. Ultimately, this can lead to gender bias, despite organisational policy and guidance claiming the contrary. Hence, my recommendation is that gender mainstreaming policy is embraced enthusiastically and adopted comprehensively across higher education, that practice is changed so that positive action measures are implemented and embedded, and that as a result this agenda is pursued rigorously.

7.2.3   Recommendation three: Further research commissioned at national level (fixing the knowledge)

- Collaborative research is commissioned at national rather than institutional level and that this research informs positive action which will bring about step change.

This recommendation focuses on further research which will enhance the attention now being given to the underrepresentation of women at the top of higher education institutions. In the years since I started my research project far more attention is being paid to my overarching enquiry 'why are there so few women vice chancellors' by a host of interested parties. Alongside this is the growing discourse both around the lack of women at the top in all sectors and also around what can be done to change things. Consequently, the conference hosted by Lancaster University in June 2013 on the theme of my PhD research 'the missing women in higher education leadership' was well attended and attracted media attention (Times Higher Education, 22–28 August 2014).

Higher education is forming and being formed by the discourse about 'the missing women at the top' and as such has a pivotal and high profile role to play. It is imperative that this momentum gains ground and that the lack of leadership diversity is tackled. For a sector whose reputation relies upon high quality research I find it surprising that major funding is not available for substantial work on this issue to continue. Piecemeal research is ongoing but researchers in this field are often dependent on small grants which are commissioned at the local level or which, by the very nature of the funding process, can encourage competition rather than collaboration. Consequently, not only it is often difficult to find out about contemporary research in this field but also to profile your own research on the national stage.

Occasionally throughout this book I have declared my interest in conducting further research related to this study. For example: exploring imposter syndrome; considering the impact of women leaders' experience of all male environments in their formative years; femininities and ambition; researching some of the men at the top and men's contribution to the gender equality agenda; and women's support for other women. These issues, along with many others, may be better researched at a macro level thereby leveraging significant funding and support. Currently I am involved in a regional study where we are researching women in the professoriate and are hopeful that the scoping study will be extended through national funding.

Thus, I recommend that collaborative research is commissioned at national rather than institutional level and that this research underpins positive action initiatives and interventions. For example, so many of the national higher education stakeholders are interested in this work now that there must be potential for them all to contribute to a body of research which has lasting and pioneering reach. In the comparatively short time I have been researching this issue many higher education organisations have shown interest in my work – ECU, Economic and Social Research Council (ESRC), HEFCE, HESA, LFHE, Society for Research in Higher Education (SRHE), UCEA, and University and College Union (UCU) – and I suggest that some mechanism is introduced which enables these bodies to pool their resources so that major funding is made available at a national level to tackle this important, universal issue. We can learn from Norway's BALANSE programme (Rustad and Ryste, 2010) and seriously profile the underrepresentation of women at the top of UK higher education and to bring the interested parties together to find solutions. In a sector with a 'thought leadership' agenda and with an abundance of intellectual capacity it is shameful that there has been relatively slow progress. Thankfully the 2015 funding letter from the Department for Business Innovation and Skills to HEFCE says 'equality and diversity are vital at all levels, not just admissions, but also in senior leadership'.

To summarise, I propose three recommendations:

- Women-only leadership education policy and practice across higher education are informed by a major evaluation study.
- Both gender mainstreaming policy and gender analysis practice are adopted comprehensively across higher education.
- Collaborative research is commissioned at national rather than institutional level and that this research informs positive action which will bring about step change.

7.3   Postscript

I have had the absolute privilege to continue my research into the women missing from higher education leadership since being awarded my PhD as part of my senior research fellowship work around gender and leadership with Leeds University Centre for Interdisciplinary Leadership (LUCILE). We hope to be publishing our research with women professors across three 'Russell Group' universities very soon at the same time as expanding this project with institutions across the country alongside an international collaboration with the women in higher education management network (WHEM).

References

Aaltio, I., Mills, A. & Helms Mills, J. 2002. Exploring Gendered Organisational Cultures. *Culture and Organisation*, 8, 77–79.

Acker, J. 1992. Gendering Organizational Theory. *In:* Mills, A. J. and Tancred, P. (eds.) *Gendering organizational analysis.* London, Sage, 160–248.

Acker, J. 2006. Inequality Regimes. *Gender & Society*, 20, 441–464.

Acker, S. 1992. New Perspectives on an Old Problem: The Position of Women Academics in British Higher Education. *Higher Education*, 24, 57–75.

Acker, S. 2010. Gendered Games in Academic Leadership. *International Studies in Sociology of Education*, 20, 129–152.

Acker, S. 2014. A Foot in the Revolving Door? Women Academics in Lower-Middle Management. *Higher Education Research & Development*, 33, 73–85.

Acker, S. & Armenti, C. 2004. Sleepless in Academia. *Gender and Education*, 16, 3–24.

Acker, S. & Piper, D. W. 1984. *Is higher education fair to women?*, London, Taylor and Francis.

Ahmed, S. 1999. *Differences that matter [electronic resource]: Feminist theory and postmodernism*, Cambridge, Cambridge University Press.

Airini, E., Collings, S., Conner, L., Mcpherson, K., Midson, B. & Wilson, C. 2011. Learning to Be Leaders in Higher Education: What Helps or Hinders Women's Advancement as Leaders in Universities. *Educational Management Administration & Leadership*, 39, 44–62.

Alimo-Metcalfe, B. 2005. Leadership: A Time for a New Direction? *Leadership*, 1, 51–71.

Alimo-Metcalfe, B. 2010. An Investigation of Female and Male Constructs of Leadership and Empowerment. *Gender in Management: An International Journal*, 25, 640–648.

Allan, E. J., Iverson, S. V. D. & Ropers-Huilman, R. 2010. *Reconstructing policy in higher education: Feminist poststructural perspectives*, New York; London, Routledge.

Alvesson, M. 2002. *Understanding organisational culture*, London, Sage.

Alvesson, M. & Billing, Y. D. 2009. *Understanding gender and organizations*, Los Angeles, CA, Sage.

Bagilhole, B. 2007. Challenging Women in the Male Academy: Think About Draining the Swamp. *In:* Cotterill, P., Jackson, S. and Wetherby, G. (eds.) *Challenges and negotiations for women in higher education*, Kluwer, Springer.

Bagilhole, B. & White, K. 2011. *Gender, power and management [electronic resource]: A cross-cultural analysis of higher education*, Basingstoke, Palgrave Macmillan.

Bagilhole, B. & White, K. (eds.) 2013. *Generation and gender in academia*, London, Palgrave Macmillan.

Balbus, I. 1987. Disciplining Women: Michel Foucault and the Power of Feminist Discourse. *In:* Cornell, S. B. D. (ed.) *Feminism as Critique,* Cambridge, Polity Press.

Barry, J., Dent, M. & O'Neill, M. (eds.) 2003. *Gender and the public sector: Professionals and managerial change*, London, Taylor & Francis.

Bascom-Slack, C. A. 2011. Balancing Science and Family: Tidbits of Wisdom from Those Who've Tried It and Succeeded. *The Yale Journal of Biology and Medicine*, 84, 219–225.

Bates, L. 2014. *Everyday sexism*, New Delhi, Simon & Schuster.

Baxter, J. 2011. Survival or Success?: A Critical Exploration of the Use of 'Double-Voiced Discourse' by Women Business Leaders in the UK. *Discourse & Communication*, 5, 231–245.

Beard, M. 2014. The Public Voice of Women. *The London Review of Books* [Online]. Available: http://www.lrb.co.uk/v36/n06/mary-beard/the-public-voice-of-women/ [Accessed 20 May 2014].

Bebbington, D. 2012. Revisiting Diversity in Leadership. *In Practice*, issue 31. London, Leadership Foundation for Higher Education.

Behar, R. 1997. *The vulnerable observer: Anthropology that breaks your heart*, England, Beacon Press.

Bell, C., Hegarty, A. & Livingstone, S. 1996. The Enduring Controversy: Developments in Affirmative Action Law in North America. *International Journal of Discrimination and the Law*, 1, 233–260.

Bendl, R. & Schmidt, A. 2013. Gender Mainstreaming: An Assessment of Its Conceptual Value for Gender Equality. *Gender, Work & Organization*, 20, 364–381.

Benschop, Y. & Brouns, M. 2003. Crumbling Ivory Towers: Academic Organizing and Its Gender Effects. *Gender, Work & Organization*, 10, 194–212.

BERA (British Educational Research Association). 2011. *Ethical guidelines for educational research*. London, BERA.

Bertrand, M., Black, S., Jensen, S. & Lleras-Muney, A. 2014. *Breaking the glass ceiling? The effect of board quotas on female labour market outcomes in Norway.* Los Angeles, UCLA.

Bickley, M. 2010. Women in Leadership: Strategies for Change. *In:* Department for Communities, W. S. I., Government of Western Australia. (ed.) Western Australia, Curtin University.

Bielby, W. T. 2000. Minimizing Workplace Gender and Racial Bias. *Contemporary Sociology*, 29, 120–129.

Bilge, S. 2010. Recent Feminist Outlooks on Intersectionality. *Diogenes*, 57, 58–72.

Bilimoria, D. & Piderit, S. K. 2007. *Handbook on women in business and management*, Cheltenham, UK, Edward Elgar Publishing.

Bilimoria, D. & Wheeler, J. V. 2000. *Women corporate directors: Current research and future directions*, London, Sage Publications Ltd.

Bird, S. R. 2011. Unsettling Universities' Incongruous, Gendered Bureaucratic Structures: A Case Study Approach. *Gender, Work & Organization*, 18, 202–230.

Bourdieu, P., Calhoun, C. J., Lipuma, E. & Postone, M. 1993. *Bourdieu: Critical perspectives*, Chicago, University of Chicago Press.

Brannen, J. 1993. Research Note: The Effects of Research on Participants: Findings from a Study of Mothers and Employment. *Sociological Review*, 41, 328–346.

Breakwell, G. & Tytherleigh, M. Y. 2008. *The characteristics, roles and selection of vice-chancellors*, London, Leadership Foundation for Higher Education.

Brooks, A. & Mackinnon, A. 2001. *Gender and the restructured university: Changing management and culture in higher education*, Buckingham, Society for Research into Higher Education & Open University Press.

Brown, L. 2004. Diversity: The Challenge for Higher Education. *Race, Ethnicity and Education*, 7, 21–34.

Buchbinder, D. 1994. *Masculinities and identities*, Carlton, Vic. Portland, Or., Melbourne University Press; International Specialized Book Services Distributor.

Butler, J. 2006. *Gender trouble: Feminism and the subversion of identity*, New York, Routledge.

Butler, J. & Dawson, B. 2006. *Gender trouble: Feminism and the subversion of identity*, New York; London, Routledge.

Butler, S. R. 2013. *A critical mass of women on the board of directors as critical influencers*, Atlanta, Georgia Institute of Technology – Scheller College of Business.

Cabrera, E. F. 2009. Protean Organizations: Reshaping Work and Careers to Retain Female Talent. *Career Development International*, 14, 186–201.

Calas, M. & Smircich, L. 1992. Using the 'F' Word: Feminist Theories and the Social Consequences of Organizational Research. *In:* Mills, A. J. & Tancred, P. (eds.) *Gendering organizational analysis*, London, Sage.

Carvalho, T., White, K. & Machado-Taylor, M. 2013. Top University Managers and Affirmative Action. *Equality, Diversity and Inclusion*, 32, 394–409.

Cassell, C. M. & Symon, G. (eds.) 2012. *Qualitative organizational research: Core methods and current challenges*, London, Sage.

Catalyst. 2007. *The double-bind dilemma for women in leadership: Damned if you do, doomed if you don't*, New York, Catalyst.

CEDAW. 2013. *Convention on the Elimination of All Forms of Discrimination Against Women* [Online]. Available: http://www.un.org/womenwatch/daw/cedaw/ [Accessed 9 August 2013].

Chesler, P. 2001. *Woman's inhumanity to woman*, New York, Thunder's Mouth Press/Nation Books.

Chesterman, C. & Ross-Smith, A. 2005. 'Making a Demonstrable Difference': Women Executives Efforts to Redefine Higher Education Management. *In:* Maione, V. (ed.) *Gender equality in higher education*, Milan, FrancoAngeli.

Chesterman, C. & Ross-Smith, A. 2006. Not Tokens: Reaching a 'critical mass' of Senior Women Managers. *Employee Relations*, 28, 540–552.

Chesterman, C., Ross-Smith, A. & Peters, M. 2005. 'Not doable jobs!' Exploring Senior Women's Attitudes to Academic Leadership Roles. *Women's Studies International Forum*, 28, 163–180.

CIPD 2005. *Managing diversity: Linking theory and practice to business performance*, London, Chartered Institute of Personnel and Development.

CIPD. 2015. Gender diversity in the boardroom: reach for the top. London. Chartered Institute of Personnel and Development.

Clarke, C. & Knights, D. 2014. Reconfiguring resistance: Gendered subjectivity and New managerialism in UK Business Schools. *Organisation Studies Summer Workshop: Resistance, Resisting and Resisters in and Around Organisations*. Corfu, Greece, Open University Business School, UK.

Clarke, M. 2011. Advancing Women's Careers Through Leadership Development Programs. *Employee Relations*, 33, 498–515.

Club. 2010. *The 30% Club* [Online]. Available: http://www.30percentclub.org.uk/wp-content/uploads/2014/02/About-30pcClubFeb2014.pdf [Accessed 3 May 2014].

Coates, J. M. & Herbert, J. 2008. Endogenous Steroids and Financial Risk Taking on a London Trading Floor. *Proceedings of the National Academy of Sciences*, 105, 167–172.

Coleman, M. 2006. *Gender and headship in the twenty-first century [electronic resource]*, London, IOE.

Coleman, M. 2011. *Women at the top: Challenges, choices and change*, Basingstoke, Palgrave MacMillan.

Coleman, M. 2012a. Interviewing. *In:* Briggs, A. C. and Morrison, M. (eds.) *Research Methods in Management and Leadership*, London, Sage.

Coleman, M. 2012b. Leadership and Diversity. *Educational Management Administration & Leadership*, 40: 592–609

Coleman, M. & Glover, D. 2010. *Educational leadership and management: Developing insights and skills*, Buckingham, Open University Press.

Collins. 2013. *Collins Online Dictionary* [Online]. Available: http://www .collinsdictionary.com/dictionary/english/critical-mass?showCookiePolicy= true [Accessed 30 July 2013].

Commission, E. A. H. R. 2011. *Sex and power*, London, EHRC.

Commission, E. A. H. R. 2014. *Inquiry into the Recruitment and Appointment Practices on Company Boards* [Online]. London, EHRC. Available: http://www .equalityhumanrights.com/legal-and-policy/our-legal-work/inquiries-and -assessments/inquiry-recruitment-and-appointment-practices-company -boards [Accessed 6 August 2014].

Connell, R. W. 1987. *Gender and power: Society, the person, and sexual politics*, Stanford, CA, Stanford University Press.

Connell, R. W. 1995. *Masculinities*, Cambridge, Polity Press.

Connell, R. W. 2002. *Gender*, Cambridge, Polity Press.

Cummins, H. A. 2005. Mommy Tracking Single Women in Academia When They Are Not Mommies. *Women's Studies International Forum*, 28, 222–231.

David, M. 2014. Feminism, Gender and Universities. Farnham. Ashgate Publishing.

Davidson, M. & Burke, R. J. 2011. *Women in management worldwide: Progress and prospects*, Farnham, Surrey, Gower.

Davies, L. 2014. *Women on boards*, London, Department for Business Innovation and Skills.

Davies, M. 2011. *Women on boards*, London, Department for Business Innovation and Skills.

Dawson, J., Kersley, R. & Natella, S. 2014. *The CS gender 3000: Women in senior management*, Zurich, Credit Suisse Research Institute.

De Beauvoir, S., Borde, C. & Malovany-Chevallier, S. 2011. *The second sex*, London, Vintage.

Dean, D. R., Bracken, S. J. & Allen, J. K. 2009. *Women in academic leadership: Professional strategies, personal choices*, Sterling, VA, Stylus Publishing.

Deem, R. 2003. Managing to Exclude? Manager-Academic and Staff Communities in Contemporary U.K. Universities. *In:* Tight, M. (ed.) *Access and Exclusion*, Bingley, Emerald.

Deem, R., Ozga, J. T. & Prichard, C. 2000. Managing Further Education: Is It Still Men's Work Too? *Journal of Further and Higher Education*, 24, 231–250.

Deem, R. E. A. 2007. *Knowledge, higher education, and the new managerialism: The changing management of UK universities*, Oxford, Oxford University Press.

Deloitte. 2011. *Only skin deep? Re-examining the business case for diversity*, Sydney, Deloitte Australia.

Democracy, C. F. W. A. 2013. *Sex and power 2013: Who runs Britain?* London, Counting Women in Coalition.

Denscombe, M. 2009. *Ground rules for social research [electronic resource]: Guidelines for good practice*, Maidenhead, McGraw-Hill International (UK) Ltd.

Denzin, N. K. & Lincoln, Y. S. 2008. *The landscape of qualitative research*, Los Angeles; London, Sage.

Department for Business Innovation and Skills. 2013. *The business case for equality and diversity: A survey of the academic literature*, London, UK Government.

Derrida, J. 1976. *Of grammatology*, Baltimore, Johns Hopkins University Press.

Desvaux, G., Devillard, S. & Sancier-Sultan, S. 2010. Women Matter—Women at the Top of Corporations: Making It Happen, London; New York, McKinsey & Company.

Devillard, S., Sancier, S., Werner, C., Maller, I. & Kossoff, C. 2013. *Women Matter 2013—Gender diversity in top management: Moving corporate culture, moving boundaries*, London; New York, McKinsey & Company.

Doherty, L. & Manfredi, S. 2006. Women's Progression to Senior Positions in English Universities. *Employee Relations*, 28, 553–572.

Doherty, L. & Manfredi, S. 2010. Improving Women's Representation in Senior Positions in Universities. *Employee Relations*, 32, 38–55.

Eagly, A. H. & Johannesen-Schmidt, M. C. 2001. The Leadership Styles of Women and Men. *Journal of Social Issues*, 57, 781–797.

Eagly, A. H. & Carli, L. L. 2007. Women and the Labyrinth of Leadership. *Harvard iness Review*, 85, 63–71.

ECU 2014. *Equality in higher education: Statistical report 2014*, London, Equality Challenge Unit.

Elliott, C. & Stead, V. 2009. *Women's leadership [electronic resource]*, Basingstoke, Palgrave Macmillan.

Elsesser, K. M. & Lever, J. 2011. Does Gender Bias Against Female Leaders Persist? Quantitative and Qualitative Data from a Large-Scale Survey. *Human Relations*, 64, 1555–1578.

Ely, R. J. 1995. The Power in Demography: Women's Social Constructions of Gender Identity at Work. *The Academy of Management Journal*, 38, 589–634.

Ely, R., Ibarra, H. & Kolb, D. 2011. Taking Gender into Account: Theory and Design for Women's Leadership Development Programmes. *INSEAD: Teaching Leadership Special Issue*, 10.

Ely, R., Ibarra, H. & Kolb, D. 2011. Taking Gender Into Account: Theory and Design for Women's Leadership Development Programmes. *INSEAD: Teaching Leadership Special Issue*, 10.

Erkut, S., Kramer, V. W. & Konrad, A. M. 2008. Critical Mass: Does the Number of Women on a Corporate Board Make a Difference? *In:* Vinnicombe, S., Singh, V., Burke, J., Bilimoria, D. & Huse, M. (eds.) *Women on Corporate Boards of Directors: International Research and Practice*, Cheltenham, Edward Elgar Publishing.

Etzkowitz, H., Kemelgor, C., Neuschatz, M., Uzzi, B. & Alonzo, J. 1994. The Paradox of Critical Mass for Women in Science. *Science*, 266, 51–54.

Eveline, J. 2005. Woman in the Ivory Tower: Gendering Feminised and Masculinised Identities. *Journal of Organizational Change Management*, 18, 641–658.

Fels, A. 2004. *Necessary dreams [electronic resource]: Ambition in women's changing lives*, New York, Pantheon Books.

Ferguson, K. E. 1984. *The feminist case against bureaucracy*, Philadelphia, Temple University Press.

Ferrary, M. 2009. *Why Women Managers Shine* [Online]. *Financial Times*. Available: http://www.ft.com/cms/s/0/27836d74-04e4-11de-8166-000077b07658.html#axzz2IFKIvoCC [Accessed 30 November 2012].

Fitzgerald, T. 2013. *Women leaders in higher education: Shattering the myths*, Abingdon, Routledge.

Ford, J., Burkinshaw, P. & Cahill, J. 2014. *White rose women in leadership initiative: Absent talent in UK HEIs?* Leeds, Leeds University Centre for Interdisciplinary Studies [LUCILE].

Ford, J., Harding, N. & Learmonth, M. 2008. *Leadership as identity: Constructions and deconstructions*, London, Palgrave Macmillan.

Ford, J. C. D. 2011. In Search of the Perfect Manager? Work-Life Balance and Managerial Work. *Work, Employment and Society*, 25, 257–273.

Forum, A. 2010. The 2010 Athena ASSET Survey. *In:* Forum, A. (ed.). London, Imperial College London; The Royal Society.

Fotaki, M. 2013. No Woman Is Like a Man (in Academia): The Masculine Symbolic Order and the Unwanted Female Body. *Organization Studies*, 34, 1251–1275.

Foucault, M. & Gordon, C. 1980. *Power-knowledge: Selected interviews and other writings, 1972–1977*, Harlow, Longman.

Jones, A. 2006. *Rising to the challenge of diversity: A discussion of the business case.* London, The Work Foundation.

Fox, S. 2006. 'Inquiries of Every Imaginable Kind': Ethnomethodology, Practical Action and the New Socially Situated Learning Theory. *The Sociological Review*, 54.

Francis, B. 1999. Modernist Reductionism or Post-Structuralist Relativism: Can We Move on? An Evaluation of the Arguments in Relation to Feminist Educational Research. *Gender and Education*, 11, 381–393.

Francis, B. 2002. Relativism, Realism, and Feminism: An Analysis of Some Theoretical Tensions in Research on Gender Identity. *Journal of Gender Studies*, 11, 39–54.

Francis, B. 2010. Re/Theorising Gender: Female Masculinity and Male Femininity in the Classroom? *Gender and Education*, 22, 477–490.

Francis, B. 2012. Gender Monoglossia, Gender Heteroglossia: The Potential of Bakhtin's Work for Re-Conceptualising Gender. *Journal of Gender Studies*, 21, 1–15.

Gatrell, C. & Swan, E. 2008. *Gender and diversity in management: A concise introduction*, Los Angeles; London, Sage.

Gherardi, S. 1995. *Gender, symbolism and organizational cultures*, London, Sage.

Gilmour, N. 2010. *RE: Why accountability is what matters: Achieving a critical mass with targets or quotas* [Online]. Available: http://www.theglasshammer.com/news/2010/01/21/why-accountability-is-what-matters-achieving-critical-mass-with-targets-or-quotas/ [Accessed 6 November 2013].

Goffman, E. 1979. *Gender advertisements*, Basingstoke, Macmillan.

Goode, J. & Bagilhole, B. 1998. Gendering the Management of Change in Higher Education: A Case Study. *Gender, Work & Organization*, 5, 148–164.

Green, J. & Thorogood, N. 2009. *Qualitative methods for health research*, London, Sage.

Grove, J. 2012. Men Seek Men for Dominant Positions: Headhunters' 'baleful influence' on Equality. *Times Higher Education*, London, Times.

Haake, U. 2009. Doing Leadership in Higher Education: The Gendering Process of Leader Identity Development. *Tertiary Education and Management*, 15, 291–304.

Hakim, C. 2011. Feminist Myths and Magic Medicine: The Flawed Thinking Behind Calls for Further Equality Legislation. *Centre for Policy Studies*, London School of Economics.

Haraway, D. 1988. Situated Knowledges: The Science Question in Feminism and the Privilege of the Partial Perspective. *Feminist Studies*, 14, 575–599.

Harding, S. 1987. *Feminism and methodology: Social science issues*, Bloomington, Milton Keynes, Indiana University Press; Open University Press.

Hearn, J. 2001. Academia, Management and Men: Making the Connections, Exploring the Implications. *In:* Brooks, A. M. (ed.) *Gender and the Restructured University: Changing Management and Culture in Higher Education*, Buckingham, Society for Research into Higher Education and Open University.

HEFCE. 2013. *UK Universities Contribute to Economic Growth* [Online]. Available: http://www.hefce.ac.uk/news/newsarchive/2013/news81928.html [Accessed 20 July 2014].

Heffernan, M. 2004. *The naked truth: A working woman's manifesto on business and what really matters*, San Francisco, CA, Jossey-Bass.

Hennink, M. M., Hutter, I. & Bailey, A. 2011. *Qualitative research methods*, Los Angeles; London, Sage.

Hewlett, S. A. & Luce, C. B. 2005. Off Ramps and on Ramps: Keeping Talented Women on the Road to Success. *Harvard Business Review*, March

Holmes, M. 2007. *What is gender?: Sociological approaches*, Los Angeles; London, Sage.

Hoskins, K. 2010. The Price of Success? The Experiences of Three Senior Working Class Female Academics in the UK. *Women's Studies International Forum*, 33, 134–140.

Houle, K. 2009. Feminist Standpoint Theory and Deconstructionism. *Frontiers: A Journal of Women's Studies*, 30, 172–193.

Hughes, C. & Cohen, R. L. 2012. *Feminism counts: quantitative methods and researching gender*, London; New York, Routledge.

Hunter, C. 2011. *Tabelle – Online Forum for Senior Women in the Civil Service* [Online]. London, Civil Service. Available: http://network.civilservicelive.com/pg/groups/539036/tabelle/?ctxt=news [Accessed 25 January 2012].

Ibarra, H., Carter, N. M. & Silva, C. 2010. Why Men Still Get More Promotions than Women. *Harvard Business Review*, September, 80–85.

Jacobs, P. & Schain, L. 2009. Professional Women: The Continuing Struggle for Acceptance and Equality. *Journal of Academic and Business Ethics*, 1, 98–111.

Jarboe, N. 2013. *Women count: Leaders in higher education 2013*, London, KPMG.

Kanter, R. 1977. *Men and women of the corporation*, New York, Basic Books.

Kelly, L., Burton, S. & Regan, L. 1994. Researching Women's Lives or Studying Women's Oppression? Reflections on What Constitutes Feminist Research. *In:* Maynard, M. P. J (ed.) *Researching Women's Lives from a Feminist Perspective*, London; Bristol, PA, Taylor and Francis.

King, N. & Horrocks, C. 2010. *Interviews in qualitative research*, Los Angeles; London, Sage.

Klenke, K. 2011. *Women in leadership: Contextual dynamics and boundaries*, Bingley, UK, Emerald Group Publishing.

Knights, D. & Kerfoot, D. 2004. Between Representations and Subjectivity: Gender Binaries and the Politics of Organizational Transformation. *Gender, Work & Organization*, 11, 430–454.

Knights, D. & Murray, F. 1994. *Managers divided: Organisation politics and information technology management*, Chichester, John Wiley & Sons.

Kramer, V. W., Konrad, A. M. & Erkut, S. 2006. *Critical mass on corporate boards: Why three or more women enhance governance*, Wellesley, MA, Wellesley Centers for Women.

Langdridge, D. & Hagger-Johnson, G. 2009. *Introduction to research methods and data analysis in psychology*, Harlow, Pearson/Prentice Hall.

Lave, J. & Wenger, E. 1991. *Situated learning: Legitimate peripheral participation*, Cambridge, Cambridge University Press.

Leathwood, C. & Francis, B. 2006. *Gender and lifelong learning: Critical feminist engagements*, London, Routledge.

Leathwood, C. & Read, B. 2009. *Gender and the changing face of higher education – a feminized future?* Maidenhead, Open University Press.

Leeds, U. O. 2013. *Equality and inclusion framework*, Leeds, University of Leeds.

Letherby, G. S. J. 2001. 'Isn't he good, but can we take her seriously?': Gendered expectations in higher education. *In:* Anderson, P. W. J. (ed.) *Identity and difference in higher education,* Aldershot, Ashgate Publishing Limited.

Lyness, K. S. & Thompson, D. E. 2000. Climbing the Corporate Ladder: Do Female and Male Executives Follow the Same Route? *Journal of Applied Psychology*, 85, 86–101.

Machado-Taylor, M. & White, K. 2014. Women in Academic Leadership. *Advances in Gender Research*, 19, 375–393.

Mackenzie Davey, K. 2008. Women's Accounts of Organizational Politics as a Gendering Process. *Gender, Work & Organization*, 15, 650–671.

Manfredi, S., Grisoni, L. & Handley, K. 2014. Gender and Higher Education Leadership: Researching the Careers of Top Management Programme Alumni. London, The Leadership Foundation for Higher Education.

Maranto, C. & Griffin, A. 2011. The Antecedents of a 'Chilly Climate' for Women Faculty in Higher Education. *Human Relations*, 64, 139–159.

Marshall, C. & Rossman, G. B. 2011. *Designing qualitative research*, London, Sage.

Martin, J. 1994. The Organization of Exclusion: Institutionalization of Sex Inequality, Gendered Faulty Jobs and Gendered Knowledge in Organization Theory and Research. *Organization*, 1, 401–431.

Martin, P. Y. & Collinson, D. 2002. Over the Pond and Across the Water: Developing the Field of Gendered Organizations. *Gender, Work and Organization*, 9, 244–265.

Martinson, J. 2012. *Seen but not heard: How women make front page news*, London, Women in Journalism.

Mauthner, M. L. 2002. *Ethics in qualitative research*, London, Sage.

Mavin, S. 2007. *Advancement through sisterhood and solidarity behaviour: Why such expectations of senior women in management?* Cheltenham, UK, Edward Elgar Publishing.

Mavin, S. 2008. Queen Bees, Wannabees and Afraid to Bees: No More 'Best Enemies' for Women in Management? *British Journal of Management*, 19, Issue supplement s1 s75–s84.

Mavin, S. & Bryans, P. 2002. Academic Women in the UK: Mainstreaming Our Experiences and Networking for Action. *Gender and Education*, 14, 235–250.

Mavin, S. & Williams, J. 2012. Women's Impact on Women's Careers in management: Queen bees, female misogyny, negative intra-relations and solidarity behaviours. *In:* Vinnicombe, S., Burke, R. J., Blake-Beard, S. and Moore, L. L. (eds.) *Handbook of research on promoting women's careers,* Cheltenham, UK, Edward Elgar Publishing, 178–195.

Maynard, M. & Purvis, J. 1994. *Researching women's lives from a feminist perspective,* London; Bristol, PA, Taylor & Francis.

Mccrudden, C. 1986. Rethinking Positive Action. *Industrial Law Journal*, 15, 219–243.

Mcelrath, K. 1992. Gender, Career Disruption, and Academic Rewards. *The Journal of Higher Education*, 63, 269–281.

Mcgregor, C. 2011. The Review of Employment Pathways for APS Women in the Department of Defence. *In:* Defence, A. G. D. O. (ed.). Australia.

Mcgregor-Smith, R. 2013. Maximising Women's Contribution to Future Economic Growth. Women's Business Council, London.

McNay, I. 1995. From the Collegial Academy to Corporate Enterprise: The Changing Culture of Universities *In:* Schuller, T. (ed.) *The changing university?* Buckingham, SRHE and Open University Press.

McNay, L. 1993. *Foucault and feminism: Power, gender, and the self,* Boston, Northeastern University Press.

McTavish, D. & Miller, K. 2009. Management, Leadership and Gender Representation in UK Higher and Further Education. *Gender in Management: An International Journal*, 24, 178–194.

Meier, K. J., Wrinkle, R.D., Polinard, J. 1999. Representative Bureaucracy and Distributional Equity: Addressing the Hard Question. *Journal of Politics*, 61, 1025–1039.

Meyerson, D. E. & Kolb, D. M. 2000. Moving Out of the 'Armchair': Developing a Framework to Bridge the Gap Between Feminist Theory and Practice. *Organization*, 7, 553–571.

Middlehurst, R. 1993. *Leading academics,* Buckingham, Society for Research into Higher Education.

Miles, M. B. & Huberman, A. M. 1994. *Qualitative data analysis,* Thousand Oaks, Sage.

Miller, K. & Clark, D. 2008. Knife Before Wife – An Exploratory Study of Gender and the UK Medical Profession. *Journal of Health Organisation and Management*, 22, 238–253.

Morley, L. 1999. *Organising feminisms the micropolitics of the academy,* Basingstoke, Macmillan Press.

Morley, L. 2003. *Quality and power in higher education,* Maidenhead, Society for Research into Higher Education & Open University Press.

Morley, L. 2005a. Sounds, Silences and Contradictions: Gender Equity in British Commonwealth Higher Education. *Australian Feminist Studies*, 20, 109–119.

Morley, L. 2005b. Opportunity or Exploitation? Women and Quality Assurance in Higher Education. *Gender and Education*, 17, 411–429.

Morley, L. 2011. Misogyny Posing as Measurement: Disrupting the Feminisation Crisis Discourse. *Contemporary Social Science*, 6, 223–235.

Morley, L. 2013a. The Rules of the Game: Women and the Leaderist Turn in Higher Education. *Gender and Education*, 25, 116–131.

Morley, L. 2013. Women and Higher Education Leadership: Absences and Aspirations. *Stimulus Paper*, London, LFHE.

Morley, L. 2014. Lost Leaders: Women in the Global Academy. *Higher Education Research & Development*, 33, 114–128.

Morrison, E., Rudd, E. & Nerad, M. 2011. Onto, Up, Off the Academic Faculty Ladder: The Gendered Effects of Family on Career Transitions for a Cohort of Social Science Ph.Ds. *The Review of Higher Education*, 34, 525–553.

Morrissey, H. & Nawrockyi, K. 2014. *Opportunity now project 28–40 the report*, London, Opportunity Now Business in the Community PWC.

O'Cinneide, C. 2012. *Positive action*, London, University College London.

O'Connor, P. 2011. *Gender and university senior management*, London, *CHES Seminar*.

O'Connor, P., Carvalho, T. & White, K. 2014. The Experiences of Senior Positional Leaders in Australian, Irish and Portuguese Universities: Universal or Contingent? *Higher Education Research & Development*, 33, 5–18.

Oakley, A. 1998. Gender, Methodology and People's Ways of Knowing: Some Problems with Feminism and the Paradigm Debate in Social Science. *Sociology*, 32, 707–731.

Oakley, A. 2000. *Experiments in knowing: Gender and method in the social sciences*, Cambridge, Polity Press.

ONS (2014) Office for National Statistics, [Online]. Available: http://www.ons.gov.uk/ons/rel/ashe/annual-survey-of-hours-and-earnings/2014-provisional-results/pre-release-access-list–2014-annual-survey-of-hours-and-earnings-test.html [Accessed 28 January 2015].

Osmond, J. 2009. *Critical mass: The impact and future of female representation in the National Assembly for Wales*, Cardiff, Wales, The Institute for Welsh Affairs.

Paechter, C. F. 2003a. Learning Masculinities and Femininities: Power/Knowledge and Legitimate Peripheral Participation. *Women's Studies International Forum*, 26, 541–552.

Paechter, C. F. 2003b. Masculinities and Femininities as Communities of Practice. *Women's Studies International Forum*, 26, 69–77.

Paechter, C. F. 2006. Power, Knowledge and Embodiment in Communities of Sex/Gender Practice. *Women's Studies International Forum*, 29, 13–26.

Paechter, C. F. 2007. *Being boys, being girls: Learning masculinities and femininities*, Maidenhead, Open University Press.

Page, M. L. 2011. Gender Mainstreaming – Hidden Leadership? *Gender, Work & Organization*, 18, 318–336.

Parsons, E. & Priola, V. 2013. Agents for Change and Changed Agents: The Micrpolitics of Change and Feminism in the Academy. *Gender, Work & Organization*, 20, 580–598.

Pateman, C. 1988. *The sexual contract*, Stanford, Stanford University Press.

Patton, M. Q. 2002. *Qualitative research and evaluation methods*, Thousand Oaks, Sage.

Perry, G. 2014. *The rise and fall of Default Man. New statesman*, London, New Statesman Limited.

Peterson, H. 2014. An Academic 'Glass Cliff'? Exploring the Increase of Women in Swedish Higher Education Management. *Athens Journal of Education* 1(1): 32–44.

Phillips, K. 2012. *Companies with female directors perform better*. HR review, London, Black and White Trading Limited.

Prasad, P. 1997. *Managing the organizational melting pot: Dilemmas of workplace diversity*, Thousand Oaks, CA, Sage Publications.

Pringle, J. 2008. Gender in Management: Theorizing Gender as Heterogender. *British Journal of Management* 19, S110–S119.

Priola, V. 2007. Being Female Doing Gender. Narratives of Women in Education Management. *Gender and Education*, 19, 21–40.

Pritchard, R. O. 2010. Attitudes to Gender Equality Issues in British and German Academia. *Higher Education Management and Policy*, 22, 1–24.

Prosser, M. 2006. *Shaping a fairer future*, London, Department of Trade and Industry.

Puwar, N. 1997. Reflections on Interviewing Women MPs. *Sociological Research Online* [Online], vol. 2 Available: http://socresonline.org.uk/2/1/4 .html [Accessed 17 March 2012].

Reay, D. 1996. Insider Perspectives or Stealing the Words Out of Women's Mouths: Interpretation in the Research Process. *Feminist Review: Speaking Out: Researching and Representing Women*, 53, 55–71.

Reinharz, S. & Davidman, L. 1992. *Feminist methods in social research*, New York, Oxford University Press.

Rice, C. 2014. *6 steps to gender equality: How every university can get more women to the top and why they should*, Tromso, Science in Balance Group.

Ross, H. 2008. Proven Strategies for Addressing Unconscious Bias in the Workplace. *CDO Insights*, 2, 1–20.

Ross, R. & Schneider, R. 2014. *The rationale for equality and diversity: How vice chancellors and principals are leading change*. London, Equality Challenge Unit.

Ross-Smith, A. & Kornberger, M. 2004. Gendered Rationality? A Genealogical Exploration of the Philosophical and Sociological Conceptions of Rationality, Masculinity and Organization. *Gender, Work & Organization*, 11, 280–305.

Rugg, G. & Petre, M. 2007. *A gentle guide to research methods*, Maidenhead, Open University Press.

Rustad, L. M. & Ryste, M. E. 2010. Talent at Stake: Changing the Culture of Research – Gender Sensitive Leadership. Committee for Gender Balance and Diversity in Research, Oslo, Norwegian Ministry of Education and Research, 1–72.

Ryan, M. K. & Haslam, S. A. 2005. The Glass Cliff: Evidence That Women Are Over-Represented in Precarious Leadership Positions. *British Journal of Management*, 16, 81–90.

Ryan-Flood, R. & Gill, R. 2010. *Secrecy and silence in the research process: Feminist reflections*, Abingdon, Oxon; New York, NY, Routledge.

Sandberg, S. 2013. *Lean in: Women work and the will to lead*, New York, Random House.

Saunders, K., Willemsen, T. M. & Millar, C. J. M. 2009. Views from Above the Glass Ceiling: Does the Academic Environment Influence Women Professors' Careers and Experiences? *Sex Roles*, 60, 301–312.

Saunderson, W. 2002. Women, Academia and Identity: Constructions of Equal Opportunities in the 'New Managerialism'– A Case of 'Lipstick on the Gorilla'? *Higher Education Quarterly*, 56, 376–406.

Schein, V. E. & Davidson, M. J. 1993. Think Manager, Think Male. Management Development Review 05/1993 6(3).

Schein, V. E., Mueller, R., Lituchy, T. & Liu, J. 2006. Think Manager – Think Male: A Global Phenomenon? *Journal of Organizational Behavior*, 17, 33–41.

Schiebinger, L. 1999. *Has feminism changed science?*, Cambridge, MA, Harvard University Press.

Senge, P. 1990. *The fifth discipline: The art and practice of the learning organization*, New York, Doubleday.

Skeggs. B. 1994. Situating the Production of Feminist Ethnography. *In:* Maynard, M. P. J. (ed.) *Researching Women's Lives from a Feminist Perspective*, London, Bristol, PA, Taylor and Francis.

Skeggs, B. 2004. *Class, self, culture*, London; New York, Routledge.

Smulyan, L. 2004. Redefining Self and Success: Becoming Teachers and Doctors. *Gender and Education*, 16, 225–245.

Soper, K. 1990. *Troubled pleasures: Writings on politics, gender and Hedonism*, London, Verso.

Spar, D. L. 2012. The woman's problem. *Harvard magazine*, Harvard, Harvard University.

Spender, D. 1981. *Men's studies modified: The impact of feminism on the academic disciplines*, Oxford, Pergamon.

Spradley, J. P. 1979. *The ethnographic interview*, New York, Holt.

Sprague, J. 2013. The Academy as a Gendered Institution. *Warwick University Feminism Conference*. Warwick.

Stead, V. 2013. Learning to Deploy (in)visibility: An Examination of Women Leaders' Lived Experiences. *Management Learning*, 44, 63–79.

Sturges, J. 1999. What It Means to Succeed: Personal Conceptions of Career Success Held by Male and Female Managers at Different Ages. *British Journal of Management*, 10, 239–252.

Talent, T. 2014. *The career paradox for UK women*, Oxford, Talking Talent.

Tierney, W. G. 1988. Organizational Culture in Higher Education: Defining the Essentials. *Journal of Higher Education*, 59, 2–21.

Tiessen, R. 2007. *Everywhere/nowhere. gender mainstreaming in development agencies*, Connecticut, Kumarian Press.

Torchia, M., Calabrò, A. & Huse, M. 2011. Women Directors on Corporate Boards: From Tokenism to Critical Mass. *Journal of Business Ethics*, 102, 299–317.

UCU 2013. *The position of women and BME staff in professorial roles in UK HEIs.* London, UCU.

UN (United Nations) Women. 2014. *He for She* [Online]. Available: http://www.heforshe.org/ [Accessed 1 November 2014].

van den Brink, M. 2011. Scouting for Talent: Appointment Practices of Women Professors in Academic Medicine. *Social Science & Medicine*, 72, 2033–2040.

Van den Brink, M. B. Y. 2012. Slaying the Seven-Headed Dragon: The Quest for Gender Change in Academia. *Gender, Work & Organization*, 19, 71–92.

Van den Brink, M. S. L. 2009. Doing Gender in Academic Education: The Paradox of Visibility. *Gender, Work & Organization*, 16, 452–470.

Vinnicombe, S., Doldor, E. & Turner, C. 2014. *The female FTSE board report 2014: Crossing the finishing line*, Bedford, UK, Cranfield International Centre for Women Leaders.

Vinnicombe, S., Singh, V., Burke, R. J., Bilimoria, D. & Huse, M. 2008. *Women on corporate boards of directors*, Cheltenham, UK, Edward Elgar Publishing.

Wagner, A., Acker, S. & Mayuzumi, K. 2008. *Whose university is it, anyway?: Power and privilege on gendered terrain*, Toronto, Sumach Press.

Wajcman, J. 1998. *Managing like a man: Women and men in corporate management*, Cambridge, Polity.

Wakefield, S. 2014. *The G20 and gender equality*, Oxford, Oxfam International.

Walby, S. 2011. Women are Crucial to Economic Recovery. *Knowledge Economy* [Online]. Available: http://www.theworkfoundation.com/pressmedia/blogs/blog.aspx?oItemId=484 2012 [Accessed 7 April 2013].

Walford, G. 2011. Researching the Powerful. [Online]. Available: http://www.bera.ac.uk/resources/researching-powerful [Accessed 20 April 2012].

Walkerdine, V., Lucey, H. & Melody, J. 2001. *Growing up girl: Psychosocial explorations of gender and class*, Basingstoke, Palgrave.

Warwick, D. 2004. Women and Leadership: A Higher Education Perspective. University of Westminster. A speech given at the Barbara Diamond Memorial Lecture, London.

Wenger, E. 1998. *Communities of practice: Learning, meaning, and identity*, Cambridge, Cambridge University Press.

Wenger, E., Mcdermott, R. A. & Snyder, W. 2002. *Cultivating communities of practice [electronic resource]: A guide to managing knowledge*, Boston, MA, Harvard Business School Press.

West, C. & Zimmerman, D. 1987. 'Doing gender'. *Gender & Society*, 1, 125–151.

Wharton, A. S. 2005. *The sociology of gender: An introduction to theory and research*, Malden, MA, Blackwell Publishing.

Wharton, A. S. 2012. *The sociology of gender: An introduction to theory and research*, Oxford, Wiley-Blackwell.

Wicks, D. & Bradshaw, P. 2002. Investigating gender and organisational culture. *In:* Aaltio, I. & Mills, A. J. (eds.) *Gender, identity and the culture of organisations,* London, Routledge.

Wiles, R., Crow, G., Heath, S. & Charles, V. 2006. Anonymity and confidentiality. *ESRC Research Methods Festival.* Oxford. ESRC National Centre for Research Methods Working Paper Series 2/06.

Williams, K. 1989. Researching the Powerful: Problems and Possibilities of Social Research. *Crime, Law and Social Change*, 13, 253–274.

Wise, S. 1997. What Are Feminist Academics for? *In:* Stanley, L. (ed.) *Knowing Feminisms: On Academic Borders, Territories and Tribes*, London, Sage Publications.

Wynn, A. 2012. Seeing Through the Glass Ceiling. [Online]. Available: http://gender.stanford.edu/news/2012/seeing-through-glass-ceiling-1 [Accessed 15 February 2013].

Yakaboski, T. 2011. 'Quietly Stripping the Pastels': The Undergraduate Gender Gap. *The Review of Higher Education*, 34, 555–580.

Zehner, J. & Basch, L. 2009. *Women in fund management: A road map to achieving a critical mass and why it matters*, New York, National Council for Research on Women.

Index

Printed and bound by CPI Group (UK) Ltd, Croydon, CR0 4YY